Hide and Seek

Exposing the Lies in Our Belief System

Todd Mozingo

Dedication

This book is dedicated first to my loving, supportive, beautiful wife Jan. She has walked with me through some major trials and always stood by my side, and she has an incredible strength that comes from the Spirit that lives within her. Secondly, I dedicate this book to my daughters, Brianne and Brittney, who are amazing and powerful women of God. I feel secure knowing they are the future leaders of the church.

Contents

Introduction

There are lies that I believe. The problem is, I don't know they are lies. They're simply untruths I've been taught to believe that are hiding in my belief system. But I have been deceived into adopting these lies as truth, and since I operate out of what I believe to be truth, I am operating out of lies. Intriguing. And if that is not enough to melt your mind, the daunting fact is, that because I do not *recognize* them as lies, it's possible for me to live according to those lies for years and years and years!

For most of my life, I thought God wanted me to be a strong, unemotional conqueror. I really believed that because that's how I saw *Him* – that's who He was – He must expect the same thing of me. So I processed through my life doing the only thing that made sense to me, leading. But to me, being a good leader meant not getting caught up in feelings, not letting others sway my opinion, taking the bull by the horns when no one else would. And this, I believed, was pleasing to God. Why? Because God was my father and fathers are not emotional people, they're people who expect you to be strong and unemotional, to be a victor and a champion. This, certainly, was a lie I believed.

So how did this lie become rooted in my belief system? What made this deception seem like truth to me? As often times happens, this idea was firmly planted in me early on and remained a stronghold for many years.

My dad raised me without personal affection. He wanted me to be someone people would follow, strong, and unemotional. As far as my dad knew, this is what men did. This was who men were. So I believed that all fathers were like my dad, including my heavenly Father. He didn't "love" me in an emotional sense. He *is* love, therefore, He loved me, but not in an affectionate way. I knew His love was a choice, but I also believed that as my Father, He was required to love me. And what I thought He wanted from me in return was for me to be a strong leader who didn't let emotions get in the way of or be a part of who I was as a man. I was almost forty years old before I found out I had been believing a lie, and that God not only affectionately loved me, but that I could love Him back in the same way. He actually encourages that!

Satan was responsible for having hidden this lie in my belief system. It was not truth and, therefore, it was not of God. But once I found this lie in my belief system and exchanged it for the truth, I was a different man; I was a different father, a different husband, and a different leader. Love has a funny way of changing you.

I think of people in the Bible who were operating out of a lie, but because they did not recognize the lie as being one, they lived and functioned based on whatever that deception was, and it caused chaos in their lives. King Saul comes readily to mind.

King Saul was anointed of God (by Samuel) to be King and, thus, everyone recognized him as King. There was never any doubt that God had selected Saul to be King. There was never any doubt God had instructed Samuel to anoint him King. None of this was ever in doubt; Saul had clearly been chosen by God to be King, and he was. So wouldn't you think

King Saul would have operated out of the truth that his kingship was *appointed* by God, and that truth would never come into question? It is interesting, but it didn't work that way for Saul. He heard the people talk about what a great battle warrior David was, and inside the King, this translated as a threat to his kingship. We are talking about the very kingship God decreed! Now you would think that if God chose you to be King, you would have nothing to worry about when it came to fulfilling that role.

So, why *did* Saul feel threatened by David? There was a lie in King Saul's belief system. Somewhere inside him, there was a voice telling the King that David was a serious threat to his kingship. As a matter of fact, the voice was telling him that David was so dangerous the appropriate thing to do would be to kill him. What kind of lie was King Saul believing that would turn him into a murderer?

Perhaps Saul believed he was unworthy. Or maybe there was some kind of fear inside of him. Maybe Saul was just prideful enough to believe he'd become King without God's hand. The Bible is not clear on what lies Saul believed, but his actions indicate that whatever those lies were, they were so strong within him that they led him to attempted murder. You have to be pretty convinced of the truth of something for it to drive you to that extreme, and the lies Satan planted in Saul about David drove him to that kind of desperation. This story about King Saul demonstrates the kind of chaos that can result from us basing our actions on the lies we believe.

There are still some lies in my belief system. I know this because everything I do in life is evidence of either my believing a lie of Satan or knowing the truth of God, and not all of my actions yet line up with God's character and truth. But with the help of the Holy Spirit I can shine a light on Satan's lies, and replace those strongholds with the truth of God, and once his hiding place is revealed he can hide there no more.

I am the seeker in my own game of Hide and Seek, and I'm going after those lies one by one.

Let the game begin!

One

Hide and Seek

When we were kids we played a game called Hide And Seek. It's a pretty simple game. One person covers his eyes and counts to a particular number, let's say 50, while the other players in the game find places to hide. Once the counter reaches the final number it is his job to go look for the people hiding, and if you are one of those people you try very hard to find a creative place to hide because the only way to win the game is to not be found. If you're able to find a hiding place the seeker would never think to look, at some point he gives up, and you win. But, if you are found, something very unique happens. The place you were hiding is now no longer a good place to hide no matter how creative it was because, if you played another round of the game, the person seeking would always go look where you'd hidden the last time to see if you were there again. In other words, the hiding place that is exposed is never a good hiding place again.

So, the lesson we learn from Hide and Seek — once a hiding place has been exposed, the seeker will always check that place first to make sure it is not being used again. Why is that critical to Christianity? Because the enemy finds hiding places in our belief systems. He hides there in order to influence and cause chaos in what we believe. If we cannot find him in his hiding place, he wins. But, if we can find him and expose the place he's been hiding, he can never hide there again. Let me show you what I mean in scripture:

> *Now I, Paul, myself urge you by the meekness and gentleness of Christ—I who am meek when face to face with you, but bold toward you when absent! I ask that when I am present I need not be bold with the confidence with which I propose to be courageous against some, who regard us as if we walked according to the flesh. For though we walk in the flesh, we do not war according to the flesh, for the weapons of our warfare are not of the flesh, but divinely powerful for the destruction of fortresses (strongholds).* **We are destroying speculations and every lofty thing raised up against the knowledge of God, and we are taking every thought captive to the obedience of Christ,** *and we are ready to punish all disobedience, whenever your obedience is complete.*
>
> (2 Corinthians 10:1-6, emphasis added.)

So let's look at some of the components of this scripture. The word "fortress" in the Greek is *okhuroma* (Strong's G3794), and means a castle, stronghold or a fortress. We know that people used these castles and fortresses – which sometimes were nothing more than a cave, a rock dwelling or some other kind of impenetrable place in which to hide – to protect and defend themselves from their enemies. This word in Hebrew (*metsad*) is used in:

1 Samuel 23:14 -- David hid in the strongholds in the wilderness.

Judges 6:2 -- Israel hid in dens, caves and strongholds from Midianites.

2 Chronicles 11 -- Rehoboam fortified his strongholds and hid from the enemy.

Our enemy, Satan, will also use a fortress as a place to hide, and once we've allowed him to build a stronghold in our belief system he uses it to defend himself — not from us, because in reality we are not Satan's enemy, but – from God. You see God is Satan's enemy, not us. Satan is competing with God for control of our lives. Therefore, he hides lies in our belief systems in order to use any authority we may have given him to keep us from believing and surrendering to the truth of God.

So a spiritual definition of a stronghold is a hiding place for a lie of the enemy within what we believe. But we know that God offers us the truth through Jesus Christ. John 8:32 tells us plainly...

And you will know the truth, and the truth will make
you free.

So if truth brings about freedom for the believer, then what does a lie bring? Captivity. These lies that we've been deceived into believing keep us captive in the stronghold where the enemy is hiding and away from the truth of God.

Consider this -- what lie did Eve believe?

For God knows that in the day you eat from it your
eyes will be opened, and you will be like God, knowing
good and evil.

(Genesis 3:5.)

7

The lie she was sold was that she would be like God. Have you noticed that scripture says Eve was deceived?

And it was not Adam who was deceived, but the woman being deceived, fell into transgression.

(1 Timothy 2:14.)

Eve was deceived. She believed a lie. Adam was not deceived. What? Adam was not deceived; he knew it was wrong. But because she was deceived, Eve decided it was okay to eat from the tree. Let me show you more on this.

When the woman saw that the tree was good for food and that it was a delight to the eyes, and that the tree was desirable to make one wise, she took from its fruit and ate; and she gave also to her husband with her, and he ate. Then the eyes of both of them were opened, and they knew that they were naked; and they sewed fig leaves together and made themselves loin coverings.

(Genesis 3:6-7.)

Why does verse 7 begin with the word *then*? "Then, the eyes of both of them were opened..." In other words, Eve's eyes were not opened when she ate the fruit. It was not until Adam ate the fruit that their eyes were opened. Why? Because Eve was deceived and Adam was not. Adam sinned knowingly. Was it still sin for Eve? Yes, but she was deceived by the enemy into thinking it was an okay thing to do. She had a lie in her belief system – the lie that it was okay to eat this and become like God.

But again, we know that God offers us truth through Jesus Christ.

In this counter example, Jesus shows us how to not be deceived by a lie. He takes Satan right back to the origin of truth -- God.

And he led Him up and showed Him all the kingdoms of the world in a moment of time. And the devil said to Him, "I will give You all this domain and its glory; for it has been handed over to me, and I give it to whomever I wish. Therefore if You worship before me, it shall all be Yours." Jesus answered him, "It is written, 'You shall worship the Lord your God and serve Him only.'"

(Luke 4:5-8.)

The lie Satan wanted Jesus to believe here is that what Satan had to offer Jesus was better than what God had for Him. Satan was trying to convince Jesus that to have dominion over the earth was a great prize. Consider that! Why would Jesus settle for what Satan was offering Him, dominion over the created earth, when God was going to give Jesus ALL authority on earth and in heaven? Listen, Satan is always offering you less than what God has planned for you, and trying to deceive you into accepting it. If he accomplishes the deception, Satan has set up a stronghold through the lie that you believe. Let me give you a couple of examples:

– *I am not good enough for God to love me.* LIE. Jesus makes you righteous before God ... (2 Cor. 5:21).

– God does not know or care about me. LIE. He knows the number of hairs on your head ... (Luke 12:7).

– I cannot move in the things of the Spirit like others do. LIE. To each one a gift is given for the common good...

(1 Cor. 12:7).

I believe strongholds are built in us and formed over time. 2 Corinthians 10:4-5 tells us there are four progressive steps or levels to a lie as it becomes established in our belief system: strongholds/fortresses, speculations, lofty things and our thoughts.

> **- Thoughts** – In this progression, thoughts are first. What is a thought? Anything we can think about. We all have thoughts.

For as a man thinks within himself, so he is.
(Proverbs 23:7.)

Thoughts have consequences; they can lead to a positive or a negative reaction. Thoughts are the inception of the things that we end up believing, therefore, it becomes critical that we take them captive to the obedience of Christ. In other words, my thoughts have to come into agreement with the things of Christ. If my thought is lustful, it is not in obedience to Him, and needs to be held captive. If my thought is loving, then it is obedient to the things of Christ and can be released and is of value.

> **- Lofty things** -- Second in the progression. Notice that the scripture says lofty things are "raised up against the knowledge of God."

10

This is when I take my thoughts and I challenge the knowledge or words of God with my thinking. In other words, "God, you say this. But my thought is different, so I'm challenging what you say!" An example would be, Jesus said He is the way, the truth and the life and no one comes to the Father except through Him. But I think that is an unfair position. I think there should be other ways, for example through Buddha or Hindu gods. Therefore, it is valid for me to challenge what God says because I think it is unfair for the only path to be through Jesus. I am raising my personal opinion and evaluation of something over God's word rather than recognizing His word is true. I am choosing to not take my thought captive to Christ and instead challenge what God says. Now let me clearly say here that questioning God's word can be a perfectly healthy and honest place to be, and is not bad in and of itself. It is often part of our learning process. But because strongholds are formed by the elevation of our thoughts above those of God's, when we have questions, which we surely will, we need to say, "God, I do not understand, so please teach me," and refer back to God's word for the answer. Every answer we need is in God's word, and this is part of the process of taking thoughts captive to Christ.

All Scripture is inspired by God and profitable for teaching, for reproof, for correction, for training in righteousness; so that the man of God may adequate, equipped for every good work.

(2 Timothy 3:16-17.)

11

It is a dangerous path to be on when we ignore His word and carry on with our own lofty thought. Whether we have come to a place of understanding or not, we have to consider in the end that what God says is the truth.

Rather, let God be found true, though every man be found a liar.

(Romans 3:4.)

> - **Speculations** – Third. This word, "speculations," in the Greek is *logismos*. By definition it means reasoning that is hostile to the Christian faith.

In other words, we have had a thought and with it we've challenged the word of God and decided that our thought is higher than God's truth. In the former example, we believe that Jesus cannot be the *only way*. Now our thought, which turned into a lofty thing set against the knowledge of God, has progressed into a hostile reasoning against God.

> - **Fortresses/Strongholds** –The levels are complete, and the lie becomes well embedded in our belief system.

Finally, we believe the lie that there are other valid ways to get to God, not through Christ alone. We've swallowed that lie hook, line and sinker. We don't care what the word of God is, and we are declaring belief in our own conclusion regardless of what God says. That lie is so strongly entrenched in our belief system that we've now developed a stronghold where the lie will stay hidden until we expose it, making sure it cannot hide there again.

The game of Hide and Seek is on!

Another example of the progression from thought to stronghold:

> **- Thought** – God is good and yet sometimes seems angry.

> **- Lofty Thing** – God says He is love, but I think He wants to punish people.

> **- Speculation** – God forms an exclusive love club and sends other people to hell.

> **- Stronghold** – God is a mean and angry god.

Strongholds are always in conflict with what the word of God says. We may not see it, but there are lies hiding out in our nation's belief system today, and the enemy is building strongholds in our society on a regular basis. These are some of the strongholds that currently exist:

1. We are a nation that is being held captive today by our past racism – The evidence of this stronghold is that you see almost nothing in the way of solutions, only protests. From the national anthem protests, to riots against police, to the removal of statues; these are not solutions, but simply a belief that we cannot overcome the past racism. Where are the programs, training sessions, unity events, and common interest projects to bring the races together? You don't see any solutions to the current problems that may be caused by our past racism, because the lie we believe is that we're powerless to change. See how this lie brings captivity.

2. Global warming – The predominant message today is that

you are an ignoramus if you don't believe global warming is real, and that the fate of the world is in our hands. I realize this will be a controversial topic, but here is why I believe this is a stronghold. It is nothing short of arrogance to believe we can determine when the end will come to the earth. Scripture tells us that only God knows the day and the hour. (Matt. 24:35-36, Mark 13:31-32). But we believe the lie that we have the power to make the end come either sooner through neglect, or delay the earth's demise with control. It never was, nor will be, in our hands to determine!

3. Sex is an expected part of a premarital relationship – Have you ever heard the question, "How can you marry someone if you don't know what sex with them will be like?" The lie we believe is that you cannot determine compatibility without having sex with one another. In other words, you believe that all the other things you love about that person become insignificant if the sex isn't everything you want it to be, and therefore the relationship should be abandoned. And yet, the design of God is that sex is the ultimate consummation of a marriage relationship, not the premise on which it should be based. There are plenty of things my wife and I don't enjoy doing together, and yet our relationship is great! Why wouldn't I decide to try to refine that element of our relationship if it wasn't what I wanted it to be, rather than throwing the whole thing out? Think about that. I would be happy to work on improving that one aspect or any other if I loved her!

4. Grace covers sin, so it's okay to sin – This lie is permeating the church today. How did we get to the place where the very thing that separated us from a loving God in the first place, is now okay to do? Satan will lie and tell you that you

can act like the devil and receive the blessings of God. But you can theologize clear into oblivion and never get to the place where God will say, "Hey, go ahead. Play in the devil's kingdom of darkness, have a good time, it's okay with me!" Understand, I am not a legalist and I believe in the work of grace. But if the Holy Spirit is living in me, there should be a conflict that arises in my soul if I am choosing to sin. If I am doing the things that made it necessary for Jesus to die, in order to reconcile me back to God, it should not be okay. This conflict speaks loudly of what Christ did for me and that conviction draws me away from sin.

5. I am a victim of my past, and there is nothing I can do about it — We have become a society that gives favor to a victimization story. And hear me clearly: people have had some horrible tragedies in their lives and we need to be sympathetic as well as empathetic. But when your identity becomes one of a victim, it is inaccurate. Scripture is clear that we are victors, overcomers, saints, healed, and on the winning team! Therefore, we must claim who we are and stop craving the comfort that being a victim elicits. I am a man acquainted with loss and death. I know how hard life can be. But when we decide we can only remain a victim in life, we are not accepting the abundance or the identity we have been given.

6. If you do not accept the gay lifestyle you are a hater – This lie has become the mantra of anyone who wants to come against Christians who believe the bible speaks of homosexuality as a sin. The bible speaks clearly against many things as sin. I know lots of people who do many things that the bible speaks against, including sometimes,

me! I know what the bible says, and I have gay friends. Did you notice I call them friends? I don't hate them. However, I do not agree with their lifestyle before God. Does that mean I hate people who choose a gay lifestyle? No. Will I stand up for what I believe the bible says, however? Yes. Will I invite you to call out anything in me that the bible speaks against? Yes. Because I want to be in line with the word of God.

There are more lies of Satan that need to be exposed. For example:

- It is a sin according to God, but if you speak the biblical truth about it, it is hate speech.

- You cannot say anything about sin if you have sin in your life? That is hypocrisy.

- You need to tolerate whatever people want to do because it's between them and God.

And you might say, "You know, if a person believes he is a cat, you need to have kitty litter in your house when he comes over – that's the loving thing to do!" No. It's not. It's enabling perversion. And I love you cat-boy, but you are believing a lie! We need to take these thoughts into the captivity of Christ. We need to know that God offers us the truth through Jesus Christ. We must be willing to expose the strongholds, or these lies will continue to draw us into darkness and away from a loving God.

Remember, as in Hide and Seek, the devil looks for dark places to hide. But once we find those strongholds and expose them to the light, they are dismantled and rendered useless. He can never hide there again.

So how do we do that, bring down those strongholds?

Then the Lord stretched out His hand and touched my mouth, and the Lord said to me, 'Behold, I have put My words in your mouth. See, I have appointed you this day over the nations and over the kingdoms, to pluck up and to break down, to destroy and to overthrow, to build and to plant.

(Jeremiah 1:9-10.)

The key is right here in this scripture, and why we have to expose and renounce those lies and wrong thoughts. And because the thought level is actually the easiest place to stop a stronghold from forming, do it early on! Once that thought becomes a lofty thing and then a speculation, it becomes a stronghold that has made void the word of God, and we need to stop and bring it into captivity to the obedience of Christ. Then we need to shine light into that emptied stronghold and fill it with a new belief, based on the truth of God's word. It sounds simplistic, but is a critical key to removing strongholds. With the word of God planted on his lips, Jeremiah could destroy and overthrow his enemies, leaving them no place to hide.

Sanctify them in the truth; **Your word is truth**.

Two

Stronghold of Fear

In this chapter, let's talk about fear. Fear is the result of allowing a lie to invade your belief system. For example, something is threatening you, and you believe the lie that it will overtake you. But here is a truth for you: you conquered fear, it did not overcome you.

> *For God has not given us a spirit of timidity but of power and love and discipline.*
>
> (Luke 1:68-75.)

That word, "timidity" in the Greek, is *deilia*. It means fear or cowardice. When something threatens you, you develop a fear of it and a desire to retreat or run from it. But the Bible tells us something about ourselves. This Scripture says there is actually a *"spirit"* of fear, but that spirit was not given to us. So if that's true, then one thing is for sure – fear is not from God. That spirit comes from our enemy Satan, therefore, if fear enters your life it is ungodly and any decision made from that fear is an ungodly decision. When we are working in the enemy's spirit we are not conducting the business of the kingdom of God.

Once you believe a threat that has come against you and the lie of the resulting fear has entered your domain, you will have developed a stronghold in your life. So the goal is to learn, not how to fight fear, but how to keep that stronghold from developing in the first place. Remember the progression of thought, to lofty thing, to speculation, to stronghold? The first step towards the stronghold of fear starts with a thought, and as such, it can be taken immediately captive and brought into the obedience of what Christ says.

Here's an interesting fact: Did you know that seven city blocks of fog is actually equal to only one glass of water? It kind of puts things into perspective when you consider that seven city blocks of fear could be held in just one cup. So even if fear is starting to take hold, maybe worrying is not as substantial a thing as it would seem. But hear me out; if you try to fight the devil in your mind, you will typically lose, but if you fight the devil in the spirit through faith, you will always win. Why? Because fear is a spiritual matter, so you must fight spiritual things in a spiritual battle. Fear is brought on by a spirit of fear, but the spirit of truth resides inside you and will always guide you to victory when you believe that truth, rather than the lie the enemy brings.

You know, faith and fear are essentially the same thing. How can they be the same? Faith and fear are both a strong belief in something, and we develop one or the other based on what we allow into our belief system. Faith is believing in the truth that comes from God. Fear is believing in the lies that Satan tells. You probably need to go back and read those two sentences again. Listen, you can *believe* in almost anything as long as you are convinced of it, but believing a lie doesn't make it the truth. Faith is believing in the things of life which come from God. Fear is believing in the things of death which come from Satan. So if you're putting your belief in things that lead to torment and death, that is fear, it is a lie, and it is from the enemy. In the same way, as a Christian, when you put your belief in things of love and life, that is the truth, that is faith, and that is God!

So when was the first time fear was mentioned in the Bible and what can we learn from it? It all started with a God who showed His love by creating an earth and man. Everything in the garden that God created, came from Him, and all that He created came from love. For God *is* love. But there was no fear in the garden. There was no fear for man to understand, comprehend or experience. So how did it come into the picture? With sin. The love of God was rejected by man when he chose to listen to the enemy and to reject the words of God. As a consequence, sin entered the world and with it came fear. How do I know that? After sin entered and God came looking for Adam, Genesis 3:10 says that Adam hid because he was afraid. When sin, and thus fear, entered the garden, man learned to hide from the love of God. When we hide from the love of God we enable fear, and we give fear the opportunity to torment us because we are outside of His love.

> *Whoever confesses that Jesus is the Son of God* (the context is believers.) *God abides in him, and he in God. We have come to know and have believed* (faith) *the love which God has for us. God is love, and the one who abides in love abides in God, and God abides in him. By this* (God abiding in us), *love is perfected with us so that we may have confidence in the day of judgment; because as He is, so also are we in this world.*
>
> (1 John 4:15-17.)

Here we see that when we are abiding with God and He is abiding in us, we are "in" love. We are not outside the boundaries of love; we are inside of love. But do you also see what a huge statement that last verse makes? "... *because as He is, so also are we in this world.*" Wow! What is God? Love. So as He is, so also are we. We are love!

If we continue on with that scripture, verse 18 says, *"There is no fear in love; but perfect love casts out fear, because fear involves punishment, and the one who fears is not perfected in love."* So let's break that down.

There is no fear in love...

Now do not forget the context. We are talking about those who confess that Jesus is the Son of God and therefore are abiding in God.

But perfect love...

Who is perfect love? God.

...casts out fear,

So if you are abiding in God, you are inside of perfect love where there is no fear.

...because fear involves punishment.

The torment for Adam and Eve was the fear that caused them to hide from God in the garden. They were removed from God's presence and His perfect love. They were running away from that love, in fear of punishment.

The one who fears is not perfected in love.

22

Fear is the evidence of us not abiding in God.

So Satan brings torment and fear into our lives, but abiding in God casts out that fear. Abiding in God, who is love, casts out all fear because when you are abiding in love there is no condemnation, no punishment, and no torment. Conversely, abiding in fear will cast you out of love and bring torment into your life, because *in* fear, there is judgment, condemnation and punishment. Remember the garden? Man ran and hid in fear when he stopped abiding in God, and was cast out of love.

So how do we know if we are abiding in God? Look back at verse 13:

By this we know that we abide in Him and He in us, because He has given us of His Spirit. (1 John 4:13.)

We know we are abiding in God because we are abiding in His Spirit. And His Spirit is love, not fear. So if we are abiding in fear, we are not in Him, we are in hiding.

Now let me shift gears for a minute. We often have fear because we confuse facts with truth. Let me explain.

Fact: There is a tumor in my body. Truth: By Jesus' stripes we are healed. (Isaiah 53:5.) We are not living in denial. We do indeed have a tumor. But if we are walking in faith in the spiritual realm, we know that tumor has to go!

In Scripture we learn that God instituted animal sacrifices as a precursor to Christ on the cross. In other words, the sins of men were passed on to animals who were sacrificed, their blood shed daily, up until the day the perfect sacrifice, Jesus, would shed his own blood for man's sin.

*...who does not need daily, like those high priests, to offer up sacrifices, first for His own sins and then for the sins of the people, because this He **did once for all when He offered up Himself.***

(Hebrews 7:27, emphasis mine.)

But you may, as a believer, have overlooked noticing something that was clearly missing in that process. Do you ever recall reading, under the Old Covenant, that the priest would beat the lamb? Never. There was never an occasion when a lamb selected for sacrifice was beaten before it was offered up for man's sin. But we know Jesus was beaten, by orders of Pilot, before His sacrifice. Why?

But He was pierced through for our transgressions. He was crushed for our iniquities; The chastening for our well-being fell upon Him, And by His scourging we are healed.

(Isaiah 53:5.)

It's right there. Jesus was beaten *so that* we could be healed, not just forgiven. We understand that He had the wrath of God poured out onto Him for our sins, but we often overlook the fact that He took a beating so we could be healed!

How does that play into our discussion on fear? The *fact* may be that you have a tumor. The enemy will want to use that to bring fear into your life. But the *truth* of Jesus is that you *are healed*. In other words, the enemy wants you to believe in the things of torment and death, but when we abide in God, we believe in the things of love and life! Therefore, we are not afraid. Why? Because truth dispels fear.

Let me give you a truth that expels fear:

I, even I, am He who comforts you. Who are you that you are afraid of man who dies (God is asking "Why are you afraid?"), *And of the son of man who is made like grass, That you have forgotten the Lord your Maker,* (In other words, "You don't think I can help?") *Who stretched out the heavens And laid the foundations of the earth, That you fear continually all day long because of the fury of the oppressor (Satan,) As he makes ready to destroy? But where is the fury of the oppressor?* (God says, "Compared to my strength, he is nothing!")

(Isaiah 51:12-13.)

In this Scripture, God is saying, "I am the almighty creator and you are Mine! What do you have to fear? If I am on your side, how can that enemy bring you fear?"

In righteousness you will be established; You will be far from oppression, for you will not fear; And from terror, for it will not come near you.

(Isaiah 54:14.)

Fear gives the enemy strength. But because of your right standing with God, (righteousness through Jesus Christ) fear will not come near you! You will be far from oppression and terror! Why? Because you are righteous! Do you see the parallel to our earlier conversation? If you dispel fear then you will have righteousness. Fear cannot come near you if you are righteous before God.

But it gets even more exciting than that.

25

Only conduct yourselves in a manner worthy of the gospel of Christ, so that whether I come and see you or remain absent, I will hear of you that you are standing firm in one spirit, with one mind striving together for the faith of the gospel; in no way be alarmed by your opponents which is a sign of destruction for them, but of salvation for you, and that too, from God.

(Philippians 1:27-28.)

Did you notice in this verse it says, "*...which is a sign of destruction FOR THEM*"? (Emphasis mine.)

Who is them? *Them,* is your opponent; the enemy that comes against you. Listen; when you are not afraid of the enemy, you are broadcasting a message to him that he is bound for destruction! Your lack of fear reminds the demons that they are bound for hell! You see, they have no authority over you unless you give it to them!

Let's look at Jeremiah 1:9-10.

Then the Lord stretched out His hand and touched my mouth, and the Lord said to me, "Behold, I have put My words in your mouth. See, I have appointed you this day over the kingdoms (of darkness), *To pluck up and to break down, To destroy and to overthrow, To build and to plant."*

This is amazing! God is putting His words in your mouth. And with His words in your mouth you can *pluck up, break down, destroy,* and *overthrow* the kingdom of darkness in your life. In other words, you can overthrow the strongholds that are hiding in your belief system. You can expose them; you can pluck them up, break them down, destroy them and throw them out!

So what are the words God puts on our lips? Let me show you one example from the New Testament:

Blessed be the Lord God of Israel, For He has visited and accomplished redemption for His people, And has raised up a horn of salvation for us In the house of David His servant— (that is Jesus!) *As He spoke by the mouth of His holy prophets from of old— Salvation from our enemies, And from the hand of all who hate us* (that is a promise); *To show mercy toward our fathers, And to remember His holy covenant, The oath which He swore to Abraham our father, To grant us that we, being rescued from the hand of our enemies* (another promise), *Might serve Him without fear, in holiness and righteousness before Him all our days.*

(Luke 1:68-75.)

Fear contributes to our own defeat. But listen, we were made for victory! Did you see what it says in the last verse? *"Without fear!"* This is the truth of God that can be on our lips when the enemy wants to impose fear into our lives.

You have to know the truth in order to express the word of truth over fear. God has given us the truth to believe in, but when we choose fear we are believing something other than God. When we express our faith, however, it moves Him! Faith moves God. Not your fear, not your tears, not your emotions. Hear me out. What moves God into action is your faith! So the question then becomes, what is your faith in? Is it

27

in the truth of God or the lies of Satan? We must know the Word of God in order to speak the truth of God, and in the speaking of that truth, it moves God because we are repeating His Word back to Him and expressing our faith in the process. Once you know the Word of God and therefore the truth of God, you make a choice as to whom you believe – Him, or Satan.

I have been asked why I no longer fear. It's because I have a track record with God. I know His truth has prevailed in the past for me and I know it can prevail for you, if you'll just trust in His timing to overcome the enemy in your life.

Let me end with a sobering thought. Sometimes when we allow fear to take hold, we are saying to God, "I don't trust you because you are not fixing my problem right now, so I'm going to step into the enemy's camp and enable him with my fear, and stop abiding in your love because you aren't responding quickly enough." It is crazy how we enable fear when we don't trust God, and it gives the enemy full authority to torment us!

Here is a practical exercise for you. Read this Psalm and ask yourself, "Do I believe it?"

The Lord is my light and my salvation; Whom shall I fear? The Lord is the defense of my life; Whom shall I dread? When evildoers came upon me to devour my flesh, My adversaries and my enemies, they stumbled and fell. Though a host encamp against me, My heart will not fear; Though war arise against me, In spite of this I shall be confident. One thing I have asked from the Lord, that I shall seek: That I may dwell in the house of the Lord all the days of my life, To behold the beauty of the Lord And to meditate in His temple.

For in the day of trouble He will conceal me in His tabernacle; In the secret place of His tent He will hide me; He will lift me up on a rock. And now my head will be lifted up above my enemies around me, And I will offer in His tent sacrifices with shouts of joy; I will sing, yes, I will sing praises to the Lord. Hear, O Lord, when I cry with my voice, And be gracious to me and answer me. When You said, "Seek My face," my heart said to You, "Your face, O Lord, I shall seek." Do not hide Your face from me, Do not turn Your servant away in anger; You have been my help; Do not abandon me nor forsake me, O God of my salvation! For my father and my mother have forsaken me, But the Lord will take me up. Teach me Your way, O Lord, And lead me in a level path Because of my foes. Do not deliver me over to the desire of my adversaries, For false witnesses have risen against me, And such as breathe out violence. I would have despaired unless I had believed that I would see the goodness of the Lord In the land of the living. Wait for the Lord; Be strong and let your heart take courage; Yes, wait for the Lord.

(Psalm 27.)

Finally, Romans 8:38-39 says:

For I am convinced that neither death, nor life, nor angels, nor principalities, nor things present, nor things to come, nor powers, nor height, nor depth, nor any other created thing, will be able to separate us from the love of God, which is in Christ Jesus our Lord.

If abiding in God is abiding in love ... and perfect love casts out fear.... and according to these verses, nothing can separate us from God's love ... then why do we fear?

Three

Stronghold of Anger

Have you ever been angry? We all must answer yes to this question. But the Bible calls out two different kinds of anger: righteous anger, and unrighteous anger. So let's talk about the differences between them and how one can be a product of a stronghold in your life.

A righteous anger will always call out Satan or the works of Satan.

A righteous anger shows that you are defending the things of God. As an example, in Matthew chapter 21, Jesus tells the moneychangers in the temple that they have made His house, which is supposed to be a house of prayer, into a robber's den. I'm sure He did not say this calmly. Jesus recognized Satan's hand in their greed and total disregard for the purpose of the temple, and it filled Him with a righteous anger.

We see His righteous anger also when He speaks to the Pharisees in Matthew 23:15. "... *you travel around on sea and land to make one proselyte; and when he becomes one, you make him twice as much a son of hell as yourselves.*" That is a truly stiff rebuke. Even though they are converting people to a belief in God, Jesus tells them they are sons of hell. This is because the Pharisees taught people rules and regulations instead of the love of God.

In Matthew 18, we see a master forgiving a large loan to his servant, and then in turn we see that servant unwilling to forgive a small loan to his own debtor. When he finds out, Matthew 18:34 says the master was moved to anger against the servant for his unwillingness to forgive when he'd been forgiven so much. In righteous anger at his servant for not showing the same compassion and forgiveness that he had received, the master turns the servant over to the tormentors until he repays all that he owes.

But maybe we find the most supreme example in Scripture of a righteous anger, when God pours out His "cup of wrath" against sin on Jesus. We know if it is wrath from God, it is righteous.

> For thus the Lord, the God of Israel says to me, "Take this cup of the wine of wrath from My hand and cause all the nations to whom I send you to drink it."
> (Jeremiah 25:15.)

> ... he also will drink of the wine of the wrath of God, which is mixed in full strength in the cup of His anger; and he will be tormented with fire and brimstone in the presence of the holy angels and in the presence of the Lamb.
> (Revelation 14:10.)

When Jesus is in the garden of Gethsemane in Matthew 26:39 He prays, "Let this cup pass from Me." He is referring to the righteous anger God was holding against sin. On the cross, God poured that cup out on Jesus, and the beauty of that story is that Jesus took the entire wrath upon Himself so that we do not have to endure God's righteous anger.

When a cause is righteous, anger can be a very clear voice of love, and most Christian brothers and sisters need to learn to get righteously angry more often than we do. It is righteous to be angry with and rebuke the works of the enemy, as he regularly tries to kill, steal and destroy the lives of our friends and family. It makes sense to have a righteous anger against Satan for the chaos he causes in the lives of the people we love.

Listen, a righteous anger always goes against Satan and the works of Satan, not the person involved in the sin. So we have this mentality that we need to "hate the sin and love the sinner," however, in an attempt to do that we often end up becoming tolerant of the sin itself. We basically say that we are not going to be upset by what the enemy is doing; we're just going to be kind to the sinner. Being kind to the sinner may be the right thing to do, but this is a two-sided coin. The work of Satan is in play and we are not addressing that work, so in treating the person well we can let the enemy completely off the hook. Where is our righteous anger against the sin?

The question is, how do we get righteously angry at the works of the enemy and yet love our friend? It works something like this. We go to them and say, "Listen friend, I see what the enemy is doing in your life. He will, and is, deceiving you, and it will lead to chaos and destruction for you. I love you enough to pull you aside and help you see it so that together we can defeat his evil schemes." Then, in our prayer closets, we get righteously angry and declare to the enemy that we see him, we smell his foul stench, and we bind him in the name of Jesus in the life of our friend.

We've been saying that a righteous anger calls out Satan and the works of Satan. So what is an unrighteous anger?

An unrighteous anger condemns a person or the works of God. Let me say those both together. A righteous anger condemns Satan and the works of Satan. An unrighteous anger condemns a person or the works of God. So, if we have an unrighteous anger, it shows that there is something wrong inside of *us*. Our anger started with a thought that was not immediately taken captive to Christ, and it developed into a stronghold. I know that can hit hard, but it's true. Let's look at the first case of unrighteous anger in man.

So it came about in the course of time that Cain brought an offering to the Lord of the fruit of the ground. Abel, on his part also brought of the firstlings of his flock and of their fat portions. And the Lord had regard for Abel and for his offering; but for Cain and for his offering He had no regard. So, Cain became very angry and his countenance fell. Then the Lord said to Cain, "Why are you angry? And why has your countenance fallen? If you do well, will not your countenance be lifted up? And if you do not do well, sin is crouching at the door; and its desire is for you, but you must master it." Cain told Abel his brother. And it came about when they were in the field, that Cain rose up against Abel his brother and killed him.

(Genesis 4:3-8.)

The key question here is "Why are you angry?" This is the question we need to be asking ourselves. *Why* are we angry? Let's look at the sequence of events in this Scripture.

34

God tells them what kind of offerings to bring and Abel brings what God asks for. Cain does something different. God accepts Abel's offering, but rejects Cain's. Cain becomes angry and his countenance falls. God then asks him why he is angry, and tells him if he does well, his countenance will be lifted up, and if he does not do well, sin will be crouching at the door. He also tells him that sin has a desire for him and he must master it.

Please notice that God does not talk about sin prior to saying that it is crouching at the door because Cain's countenance has fallen. In other words, God doesn't tell Cain he is sinning by *being* angry. Sin enters the story only after Cain becomes angry. So God was telling Cain that there was no sin in Cain's anger itself, but that once he became angry, sin was crouching at the door and his anger could *lead* him to sin.

Be angry, and yet do not sin... (Ephesians 4:26.)

We've said that there is an unrighteous anger and a righteous anger. But the issue is not the anger itself. The issue is what is the source of the anger, and where does it lead? God is instructing Cain here that this anger, most probably unrighteous, can lead him into sin.

So, if Cain's anger itself wasn't the sin, but could potentially lead him to sin, what was the underlying root of this unwanted potential? A lie — something that started out as a thought, became elevated to a lofty thing, which turned into a speculation and then became a stronghold — ultimately becoming the source of Cain's rebellion.

When, in response to Cain's ignoring God's instructions, God had no regard for his offering, Cain became angry. Let's look at this again.

> *So it came about in the course of time that Cain brought an offering to the Lord of the fruit of the ground. Abel, on his part also brought of the firstlings of his flock and of their fat portions. And the Lord had regard for Abel and for his offering; but for Cain and for his offering He had no regard. So, Cain became very angry and his countenance fell.*
>
> (Genesis 4:3-5.)

Most scholars believe the problem was that Cain did not bring the "first" of his fruits. Notice that Abel brought the first of his flock but it does not say that Cain brought the first of his fruits. Or, a second understanding may be that he too was supposed to bring an animal sacrifice, and did not. We don't know the reason Cain decided not to follow God's instructions. Was it laziness? Was it pride? Was it just an aversion to being told what to do? The Scripture doesn't tell us. But it is not critical for us to know what the problem was, or why Cain disobeyed God's instructions, only that the result was he did not do well. Because he did not do well, Cain became angry and his countenance fell. Why did he become angry? You might answer, because God made it clear He had regard for Abel's offering but none for Cain's, and he was jealous and hurt. And you might think it was God's and Abel's fault that he felt that way. But you have to look at what God says about Cain's anger to understand where the anger really comes from. God asks Cain the question, "Why are you angry?"

Then the Lord said to Cain, "Why are you angry? And why has your countenance fallen? If you do well, will not your countenance be lifted up? And if you do not do well, sin is crouching at the door; and its desire is for you, but you must master it."

(Genesis 4:6-8.)

Look closely at the words of God. "*Why are you angry? ...If you do well, will not your countenance be lifted up?*" God is saying to Cain, "If you had done well, you wouldn't be upset. However, because you did not do well and I had no regard for your offering, you became angry." Notice God does *not* say, "When you saw what Abel brought as an offering, you got angry." And God does *not* say, "When you saw Me accept what Abel brought as his offering, you got angry." What God *does* say is, "You got angry because *you* did not do what *you* were asked to do." In other words, "Cain, this anger of yours has nothing to do with Able, or with Me. Your anger is all about you."

So had Cain not rebelled, but rather followed God's instructions, there would never have been an opportunity for him to get angry. Cain's anger is a result of whatever lie he believed which prompted him to *not* do what he'd been asked to do, which then resulted in his not doing well. Why are we making this point? Because this is how we know that unrighteous anger, which leads to sin, is typically an indication of a problem stronghold in us, not a problem in someone else. It was not Abel who made Cain angry. It was not God who made Cain angry. Cain's anger, when he did not do as God asked, was brought about solely by something that was going on inside of him. And once that anger is introduced into Cain's life, he learns that sin is crouching at the door and he must master it. Unfortunately, he does not. We know this because he eventually commits murder.

In this story, when God asks the question "Why are you angry?" God is actually saying, "Something is going on in you Cain. Anger is in you; you need to understand why. It's because you did not do well. And why did you not do well? You need to figure that out. But realize that in the state you are in Cain, sin is now crouching. It is hiding, and it's ready to pounce, and you're on the verge of walking right into it." We know scripturally that Satan roams around like a roaring lion seeking whom he may devour. And if you've watched any good wildlife shows, you've seen exactly how the lion attacks its prey. It crouches, gets very quiet, and stays there hidden until the prey comes within reach. Then, it pounces! God is trying to tell Cain, that because of his anger, he is very close to being devoured.

An unrighteous anger shows that there is something wrong in us. Inside of us, there is some lie or stronghold that we are not dealing with correctly, and as a result we step into unrighteous anger. Again, the anger is not as much of an issue as the sin that crouches at the door when we become angry. Though anger is an emotion, we need to stop focusing on the emotion itself and start looking at the source of the anger so we can keep ourselves from approaching sin. Cain killed Abel, not because of Able's offering or the subsequent rejection by God of his own offering. It was neither Abel nor God that caused Cain to kill his brother. It was the problem inside of Cain, which caused an unrighteous anger that led to his sin.

So let's look at some of the things that could be buried in us, which are often the source of an unrighteous anger, since anger is an emotion that is brought on by some-*thing*, not by some-*one*. It is not the result of another person, but of some hidden wound or lie in our heart or belief system that we don't know how to deal with. As an example, someone says something to me and in whatever they've said, there is a truth, or a lie, or a memory. That truth, lie or memory brings out anger in me because it has touched a damaged place inside me. The other person is merely the instrument that brings out the thing we don't know how to deal with, not the actual source of the anger itself.

Anger can be triggered when someone exposes and inflames hidden wounds inside us that we haven't resolved; things like feeling rejected, or the pain of having been abused or cruelly judged. Then, in response to a sore spot being touched, we lash out in bitter anger – with hatred, unforgiveness and judgment – or we respond with jealousy, hurt or offense. Now hear me out, none of these responses is about the other *person*. They are issues in *us* that bring about the anger, and they are all the result of past damage, current wounds, and lies of the enemy that are hiding in our heart and our belief system. Anger is not caused by other people, but it can be the result of any hidden wounds and hurt they have exposed. And those things need to be dealt with so that your heart does not lead you to anger and potentially into sin.

For out of the heart come evil thoughts, murders, adulteries, fornications, thefts, false witness, slanders.
(Matthew 15:19.)

What is supposed to be in my heart is the Holy Spirit and the gifts of the Holy Spirit. If, instead, there are dark things like hurts, jealousy, a need for revenge or retaliation in my heart, when someone hits one of those places anger comes out.

When I listen to other speakers, read books, or surf the Internet on this subject, I find the common approach to anger is this: we, as believers, should learn to control it. We need to count to ten. We need to do breathing exercises. We need to get away from the situation. We must capture our anger and make sure it is never released. That approach is completely wrong! It's like saying you have a wild tiger that is a ravenous killing machine. It can cause un-repairable damage and, most of the time, death when it's loose. And what you have decided to do is to keep that wild tiger in a cage. Maybe I should repeat that decision. *You have decided to keep that tiger*! What? Why would you keep a tiger that is capable of such destructive behavior? Wouldn't you spend most of your time worrying about whether or not the tiger was going to get out of that cage? You would constantly have to check to make sure it was still in there. You would regularly want to make sure the lock on the door was sound. But we need to ask the question, "Why are we keeping the tiger?" Wouldn't it make more sense to just get rid of it? Wouldn't it make sense to kill the tiger rather than constantly trying to keep it pent-up?

The answer is, yes. It *would* make more sense. So how do we kill the tiger? Stop feeding it! It feeds on evil thoughts, murders, adulteries, fornications, thefts, false witness, and slanders, among other things. This is the right approach to dealing with anger – we must get rid of its food source. We must get rid of the dark things in our heart (all lies of the enemy) that feed our anger. Our goal *has to be* to expose those lies and leave them no place to hide.

Have you ever found yourself saying something along the lines of, "We all need to vent, right? Sometimes we just need to go outside and scream, find a pillow and slug away! I need to get that aggression out?" If you've said something like that, is it because you believe if you have an outlet for your anger, you won't hurt anybody? Listen; all you are doing with any of those methods is training your anger response. You are saying, "This is what I do when I am angry. I hit, I yell, I scream, I run away." Why would we go through training to have a better *in*appropriate method of anger management, in order to deal with our anger? What we need to do is ask ourselves the question *"Why? Why* am I angry?" Because if I am, then something is broken in me. And if I can figure out what that is and fix it, anger "management" will not be necessary.

Anger is often caused by our unfulfilled desires.

What is the source of quarrels and conflicts among you? Is not the source your pleasures that wage war in your members? You lust and do not have; so you commit murder. You are envious and cannot obtain; so you fight and quarrel. You do not have because you do not ask.

(James 4:1-2.)

Did you notice the source? You lust and you do not have (your pleasures.) That is source material. And because you lust and do not have, you commit murder. Another source: you are envious and cannot obtain. And because you are envious and cannot obtain, you fight. We want something and we don't get it, so we get angry. So, when we are angry we need to stop and ask ourselves, "What do I want that I'm not getting?" But perhaps more importantly, "What is the appropriate response to not having what I want?"

For example, if a person receives something you don't think they deserve and you get angry with that person, the problem there is you! At the source, you feel shorted or rejected, maybe unrecognized or made to feel undeserving. It is time to go back and deal with that rejection and stop feeding the source, so you can be glad when others prosper. And instead of being angry, praise God they got a blessing they didn't deserve. You know, kind of like you, when you received salvation and didn't deserve it? Their prosperity is between them and God; it has nothing to do with you.

Jesus actually says that someone with anger in his heart is as guilty, if not more so, than someone who commits murder.

You have heard that the ancients were told, "You shall not commit murder" and "Whoever commits shall be liable to the court." But I say to you that everyone who is angry with his brother shall be guilty before the court; and whoever says to his brother, "You good-for-nothing," shall be guilty before the supreme court; and whoever says, "You fool," shall be guilty enough to go into the fiery hell.

(Matthew 5:21-22.)

There is a tremendous amount we can learn from this Scripture, but for the purposes of our current conversation, let's just recognize the seriousness of Jesus' view of anger. He says clearly here that there is an opportunity for sin to come out of our anger, and that sin would deem us guilty.

So let's talk about some of the lies about anger that hide in our belief system.

- Anger is an appropriate response when I do not get what I want.

- Anger is an appropriate response when I want something changed.

- It is beneficial to my wellbeing if I let myself explode, and get it all out.

- If I do explode, it is someone else's fault.

- My anger is not controllable and I am not able to do anything about it.

- My anger is not my problem; it is caused by the people around me.

- I can use my anger to manipulate a situation into becoming what I want it to be.

Let me spend a minute on that last one. For some people, anger has become their master manipulation tool, and they will use it to control a person or a situation. You see this most often in unhealthy relationships. One spouse will convince the other that holding to his or her opinion or behavior is not worth the wrath it will bring about. What I mean is that you will hear things like, "Are you trying to make me mad again?" "Do you really want to bring that up again?" "You're just asking for it, aren't you?" These are all threats. The threat is, that if you don't handle this the way I want you to, I will unleash my anger on you. And my anger is such a threat that you'd better stop doing what you are doing or I will not be responsible for my actions; whatever happens will be your fault. That is a lie straight from the pit of hell. We are all responsible for how we act and react; no one can make us do anything we choose not to do. But sometimes a pattern can develop where one spouse will submit, and enable the other by receiving the threat and allowing it to manipulate and control them. That relationship will never be good until the manipulation stops. And it stops when the angry person begins to look for the source(s) of his anger, and exposes the stronghold that is protecting those lies.

So what do we do if we struggle with anger? What do we do if we are prone to angry explosions? If we cannot keep a job or our relationships suffer because of anger? We start by evaluating what's causing that anger, get to the source of what is wrong inside us, and deal with it in the light of God's Word. Then, when we've done that, it is important that we reconcile with anyone who has been a victim of our anger. Families have often been divided for years by unrighteous anger, only because they haven't recognized that it was Satan coming against them and using anger to do it. So now that the root of the anger has been found, and the source of the problem, Satan, has been exposed, we need to apologize to family members and friends for letting our anger cause them harm. When we can *all* see Satan in unrighteous anger, then forgiveness should be available.

Recognize too, that sometimes you can justify your anger because you think it is righteous. But if it is harmful to another person, it is *un*righteous. Look at Peter's admonition of Jesus in the following Scripture:

From that time Jesus began to show His disciples that He must go to Jerusalem, and suffer many things from the elders and chief priests and scribes, and be killed,

*and be raised up on the third day. Peter took Him
aside and began to rebuke Him, saying, "God forbid it,
Lord! This shall never happen to You." But He turned
and said to Peter, "Get behind Me, Satan! You are a
stumbling block to Me; for you are not setting your
mind on God's interests, but man's."*

(Matthew 16:21-23.)

Peter has rebuked Jesus! Wow, that must take incredible
guts. But Jesus comes right back at him and says, "Get behind
me, Satan!" Well… you can say, wait! Doesn't this show Jesus
got angry with people? Jesus had every right to be angry with
Peter, because Peter was rebuking Him with something that
was contradictory to the call on Jesus' life. Peter is proposing
that Jesus not die on the cross. In other words, he was actually
speaking *against God*. But this is a very interesting comment
Jesus makes here. Did you notice He says to Peter, "Get behind
Me, *Satan!*" He doesn't say, "Get behind Me Peter!" He directs
His anger at the source of the problem, Satan, rather than
damaging Peter with His wrath. Jesus demonstrates perfectly
for us here, that Satan is the only one a righteous anger should
ever come against.

Remember, there are lies that hide in our belief system, and
these lies are not of God; they are the works of Satan. He uses
them to wound us and create chaos in our lives, and those
wounds then become strongholds that hide deep within us. We
must expose these lies and get them out of our belief system, so
he cannot continually use them against us, and those around us.

Satan offers us lies that lead to wounds that lead to
unrighteous anger, and potentially into sin. God, on the other
hand, offers us love, joy, peace, patience, kindness, goodness,

faithfulness, gentleness, and self-control. So when we get angry, it is time to look inside and ask ourselves this question — "Am I calling out the works of Satan, or condemning the works of God?"

Four

Stronghold of Depression

Many people suffer from depression, which can be brought on by a number of different things. Some people suffer around holidays, some have difficulty around dates of tragedy in their lives, and some don't know why they are depressed at all. But sometimes depression can go on for years, regardless of the cause.

We're going to talk about the stronghold of depression but before we get into this discussion, let me put a disclaimer out there. If you are on medicine for depression, for now, stay on your medicine. I fully believe God can deliver you from depression and anxiety in a mere moment. In the flash of a second that spirit of infirmity and depression can be rebuked and forced to leave you. However, I do not believe in testing God. In other words, to say, "I will stop taking the medicine as proof of my trust in God or as proof of my faith," is testing God. God may want to help you recognize the cause of the depression, He may want you to learn about the spirit that brings it about, or He may be choosing a particular time to deliver you. But the bottom line is God will tell you when to stop taking the medicine. You cannot decide for God when that moment will be.

Anxiety in a man's heart weighs it down, but a good word makes it glad.

(Proverbs 12:25.)

To grant those who mourn in Zion, giving them a garland instead of ashes, the oil of gladness instead of mourning, the mantle of praise instead of a spirit of fainting (depression). *So they will be called oaks of righteousness, the planting of the Lord, that He may be glorified.*

(Isaiah 61:3.)

This word "fainting" in Hebrew is *kaheh'*. It means dull, dim, colorless, dark – like the wick of a flame that is about to go out. According to Isaiah 61:3, this is a spirit that can come upon you. It's seems like a reasonable description of depression, right? A time when everything is dull, colorless, dark and the lights are about to be turned out. Most everything else in life ceases to matter as this feeling, this emotional state, this spirit takes over. So let's start with a very practical definition of depression.

> - Depression – A rejection of any reality, other than the dismal one in which you currently believe, regardless of the actual facts.

In other words, believing in an alternate reality, *not* the one God has defined for you. God does not give you a spirit of depression. God does not give you a life that isn't worth living, or has no hope. This depression definition does not line up with the Word of God. Therefore, if I'm believing a dismal reality, I am believing a lie.

We have already discussed that a stronghold, a lie hiding in our belief system, comes in through a progression of steps. It starts at a thought, moves to a lofty thing, then to a speculation and finally to a stronghold. Depression is one of the best examples of the stronghold four-step process. It goes like this:

- Thought –I lost my job.

- Lofty thing – I do not have an income right now. But God, you said I could have   life   and   have   it abundantly. And you said you would supply all my needs from your riches. And I am not seeing that.

- Speculation – You obviously do not care about me because you are letting me suffer. Your Word is not true for *me*, because I am struggling and you do not seem to care.

- Stronghold – God is not for me. He is against me, and punishes me unfairly.

It is really critical that we stop that process at the thought level, and go to the Word of God quickly before we move to lofty things and speculations, so we do not let it progress to a stronghold.

So let's look at a man in Scripture who went through the thought to stronghold process and ended up in a depressed state. In First Kings 19, we read one of the stories of Elijah. Most of us know this story. Elijah is telling King Ahab it is time to determine who the real God is, Baal or Jehovah God. In this showdown between Elijah and the 450 prophets of Baal, they will each build an altar and call upon their God to show himself. The prophets of Baal go first. They cry out all morning, even to the point of cutting themselves in their plea to have Baal show himself mightily. Needless to say, Baal never shows.

It is now Elijah's turn. But Elijah goes a few extra steps before he is ready to call upon God. He instructs the servants first, to bring four pots of water to pour on the altar. He does this three times. These twelve pots of water, which symbolize the twelve tribes of Israel, are a sign to the prophets that Elijah will be calling upon the God of Israel. After the water is poured on the alter, per his instructions, Elijah calls upon God. Not only does God show up, He completely consumes what is on the altar as well as the rocks of the altar, and all the water in the trench surrounding the altar, in a column of fire! After this magnificent display, Elijah proclaims it is time for the prophets of Baal to die, and he slays them all. This is a truly triumphant moment for God, for Elijah and for the Israelite nation. What an amazing display of power and of faithfulness to Elijah by God. But we pick up the story in 1 Kings 19 after these events have occurred, and King Ahab's wife Jezebel is unhappy about what has happened.

> *Now Ahab told Jezebel all that Elijah had done, and how he had killed all the prophets with the sword. Then Jezebel sent a messenger to Elijah, saying, "So may the gods do to me and even more, if I do not make your life as the life of one of them by tomorrow about this time."*
>
> (1Kings 19:1-2.)

In other words, Jezebel is saying, "Elijah, either I will die or you will die by this time tomorrow." Jezebel is making a threat to take Elijah's life. Let's continue:

And he was afraid and arose and ran for his life and came to Beersheba, which belongs to Judah, and left his servant there. But he himself went a day's journey into the wilderness, and came and sat down under a juniper tree; and he requested for himself that he might die, and said, "It is enough; now, O Lord, take my life, for I am not better than my fathers." He lay down and slept under a juniper tree; and behold, there was an angel touching him, and he said to him, "Arise, eat." Then he looked and behold, there was at his head a bread cake baked on hot stones, and a jar of water. So, he ate and drank and lay down again. The angel of the Lord came again a second time and touched him and said, "Arise, eat, because the journey is too great for you." So he arose and ate and drank, and went in the strength of that food forty days and forty nights to Horeb, the mountain of God. Then he came there to a cave and lodged there; and behold, the word of the Lord came to him, and He said to him, "What are you doing here, Elijah?" He said, "I have been very zealous for the Lord, the God of hosts; for the sons of Israel have forsaken Your covenant, torn down Your altars and killed Your prophets with the sword. And I alone am left; and they seek my life, to take it away."

(1Kings 19:3-9.)

This story has always amazed me. I see a great prophet of God who has just had a huge, monumental, historical confrontation with the King, and dramatically, overwhelmingly and convincingly won! And yet, when the wife of the King threatens his life for killing her prophets, Elijah becomes afraid and runs. Wouldn't it stand to reason that if God sent fire from heaven to consume an altar, and allowed Elijah to kill the 450 prophets of Baal, that this same God could protect him from the threat of the King's wife? But Elijah, the Scripture says, ran in fear. There in the wilderness, he tells God he is alone, that no one else is following God the way he does, and that now his life is in danger so he just wants to die. He is in a place of dimness, darkness, colorlessness, and waiting for his life to be snuffed out like a candle.

What got him to this place of despair? What can we learn from Elijah?

First, sometimes mountaintop experiences are followed by deep depressions. Elijah has sixteen miracles happen through him over the lifetime of his ministry, including raising a child from the dead! He called down a three and half year drought over the land. He has just been involved in a *spectacular* public event of power and authority, and he is now in a cave suffering from depression. What happened?

Often times when we take a major vacation, have a significant life event or succeed in some recognizable way, we then go into a valley of darkness. What happens is that we get a rush, or an emotional high from the mountaintop experience, and we enjoy it, we want it to last, we crave it. But after it is gone, we don't know how to deal with the disappointment that we no longer feel that "high." So what can we learn from this? Learn to expect the low. Learn to know that after a major event, there will come a sensation of loss. Expect that it will pass; it will be over. Learn that the enemy will come after you after a great experience. He waits to attack you until the time is right. He will choose to come after you when the moment of greatness is over and you are left with that feeling of loss. If we can anticipate this event, we can learn what to do to keep it from taking us out. If not, the following thought can become the first step towards the stronghold of depression: "If I am no longer feeling this high, there must be something wrong."

Secondly, we learn from Elijah that the words, thoughts or opinions of others can have an impact on us. They can actually assist in the stronghold process by raising our thought to a speculation. In verse one Jezebel said, "So may the gods do to me and even more, if I do not make your life as the life of one of them by tomorrow about this time."

Please hear this point: The effect someone's threatening words have on you reflects your belief of God's view of you. Here is what I mean – if another person can speak something to me and it replaces, in my view, what God thinks or says about me, I have a problem with my belief in God. I have to know who I am in Christ and who I am before God, so that I can discern the truth in what others say about me. Do you know that God loves you? Do you know that you are "hidden in Christ?"(Col 3:3.) Do you know that you are a child of God and joint heir with Jesus? (Romans 8:16-17.) You are made in His image. (Gen 1:26.) Do you know that you have authority? (Luke 10:19.)

We could go on and on about what God says about you. And they are all good things! God loves you, and guess what? God even likes you! When someone says something about you, you must measure it against what God says about you. Why? Because what God says is always truth. (Titus 1:2.) Our identity must come from God, our destinies must come from God, and our operating procedures must come from God. But the enemy wants you to believe a lie about yourself, which takes you from the thought that something is wrong, to the speculation that God does not love or support you. However, when that lie comes, if we know the Word of God we can *recognize* it *is* a lie!

Third, Elijah says, "It is enough..." Now let me ask you a question. Who is best at determining whether Elijah can handle what God has given him to do – Elijah or God? Remember that we learn from a guy in the Bible named Job, that God decides how far an enemy can come against you. (Job 1:12, 2:6.) God tells Satan there is no one else on the earth like Job. Remember *that* when you wonder if God will let Satan do to you what he did to Job. *On the entire earth, there was* no one *like Job*! Now with that said, God tells Satan, "You can take him up to the point of death but no further." So when the test is over, does Job succeed or fail? He succeeds. Why? Because God knew when it would be "enough" for Job. God determines the limits of every man. God knows how much you can take. And keep this in mind – would God chose a person to do something who would fail at doing that thing? Why would God set Himself up for failure? Why would God choose you if He did not know you could succeed? If He did, your failure could make it look as though God did not know what He was doing when He chose you. Let that sink in. Please, do not tell God that you know more about you than He does. Please do not tell God that you know more about your limits than He does.

Elijah was brought into depression by listening to his own opinion. Not only has he decided what is enough but also, in 1 Kings 19 verse 4, Elijah says he is no better than his fathers. Now he has started the comparison game. He also says, "I cannot handle this." Let me ask you another question – when you are depressed, who is absolutely the worst person to talk to? YOU! You are the worst person. Why? Because you are depressed! Depressed people make terrible counselors so stop listening to you! Why in the world, if you are depressed, would you want to seek counsel from another depressed person? Anyone would say that's crazy. But guess what? We do it all the time. We choose to listen to our own depressed counsel, even though we are the last person we should be listening to! Certainly for Elijah, listening to himself provided no comfort and no support. It was more like listening to a horrible friend who said, "You know, your dad was great, but you – eh – not so much." Or another undermining friend who said he didn't think Elijah would ever amount to much at all. That pretty much equates to saying, "I really don't see things working out in your favor, and everything is going to go quite badly." Who wants that kind of counselor? This isn't good counsel, but these are exactly the types of things we tell ourselves when we are depressed. And this is where we elevate the speculation that God does not love or support us, to the lofty thing of our *own* opinion that says we are worthless. We have now raised that up against the truth of God's opinion of us, and His love.

Fourth, Elijah takes a posture of depression. This is when the stronghold sets in. Verse 4 says Elijah went by himself and sat down. In verse 9, he went alone into a cave. For most of us men, going in to our "cave" is our first act of stupidity when we get depressed. But isolation and depression do not go together regardless of whether you are a man or a woman. From the very beginning of our existence God said it is not good for man to be alone. That still holds true today. We tend to believe that it is a good thing to be alone, hold ourselves a pity party, and ask none other than our own depressed selves for advice.

Clearly, this plan does not make sense. Listen; there is no worse place for you to be when you are depressed, than by yourself. In that place of aloneness, there is no one to give you another perspective on what is reality. And although it is clear that the Holy Spirit can give us perspective when we are alone, we tend to spend that time voicing our complaints rather than allowing Him to reveal the lies.

By the way, prayer, when you are constantly telling the Lord your problems, is not prayer; it's whining. Who wants to spend time talking to you or helping you if all you want to do is complain about how things are? God knows your needs; you do not have to tell him in fifty different ways how miserable you are. So state your case, and then listen.

Back to my point about isolation. If we were to ask any person who is not currently depressed, if it is a good idea to be alone and counseling oneself when we *are* depressed, every one of those people would say that it's a bad idea. Satan wants to get you alone. It is where he does his dirty work. It is where he tries to convince you that others are out to get you, that no one believes in you, and that you are not important or worthy. He will convince you to believe that others are plotting against you and that, for example, if they passed you in the hallway at church and did not say hi, it's because they do not like you. Satan wants you to feel hopeless, he wants you to feel lonely, and he wants you to feel condemnation. But you don't have to fall into that trap. If you are currently in a good emotional place, not depressed, and positive about your future, write yourself a note now, to keep in case a depression does come. And if and when that time comes, I hope you will recognize this advice as coming from someone you think is pretty intelligent. You!

On this note write the following:

Dear (*your name goes here*),

This is my advice:

You should have seen this coming after the mountaintop experience. Do not listen to others unless they agree with God's opinion of you. Do not take counsel from yourself; it is going to be bad advice. God knows you can handle this, He believes in you! Do not isolate yourself during this time.

Love,

(*Your name goes here*)

For Elijah, the stronghold of depression is firmly in place now and he builds an unrealistic view of things. "I am alone and they are going to kill me." Let's start with the thought, "I am alone." Listen, you are not alone, you are just by yourself and there is a difference. Being by yourself is not necessarily a bad thing, but feeling alone can be. But you are never alone. I love the way God handles it with Elijah. Elijah says basically, "I am alone and the only one serving you." God responds, "Elijah, you just missed that by 6,999."

> *Yet I will leave 7,000 in Israel, all the knees that have not bowed to Baal and every mouth that has not kissed him.*
>
> (1 Kings 19:18.)

In other words, God reminds Elijah that Elijah is not in the best position to assess who is still serving God. When he determines he is alone, God says wrong, Elijah, there are 7,000 of you! Perhaps if we listen when we feel alone, God can explain to us what the truth really is.

Some people, when they are depressed, say, "Nobody has to deal with what I am dealing with." You're wrong. Do you really believe that no one in the history of mankind, not one of the six million people currently on the planet, and not one of the people in the 66 books of the Bible ever had to deal with the same thing you are dealing with? Let me suggest that not only are you wrong about no one else dealing with it; someone else *is* dealing with that, and more! Your circumstances may be terrible, but they could actually be worse. Add to your situation cancer, a divorce, a bankruptcy, the death of a friend or family member, job loss, demonic oppression, and so on. If you are still here breathing and reading this book, it could be worse. I am well aware that the fact that it could get worse, does not make it better. It just helps put things into perspective, and suggests we may need to seek out those who have been through something similar and ask for their help.

When they are depressed, some people say, "Nobody cares." This is another lie buried in this stronghold, and here is why, when you are depressed, you believe it. You have decided *how* people should show you they care, and if no one has shown you in that way, then no one cares. The reality is that some people who care don't know how to show you they care, and some show you they care in ways you do not recognize. In either case, people do care, and are trying to show you in the only way they know how, but you are rejecting it because it is not what you were looking for. When we are depressed, we become people who say, "What have you done for me lately?"

because the measure of whether or not someone cares, is how closely they come to matching what we want them to do. We should, instead, realize and be grateful that they are trying to demonstrate they care in whatever way they can. It's truly unrealistic, unfair and unreasonable to decide that no one cares, but you can always convince yourself that is the case because people are not showing it just the way you want them to. But remember, once you instruct them as to how they should act in order to prove they care, you will most likely assume they're doing it just because you told them to, and not out of real concern. You see the catch-22? You can't trust that it is genuine because it's not *their* way; you *told* them what to do. We have to learn to recognize and accept the different ways people show their concern, in order to trust and receive it. Finally, remember that how you treat other people when it comes to showing them you care about them may be the way they show you they care when you're the one in need.

Let me illustrate how we can get caught in the stronghold of depression when we don't realize that others may not know how we *perceived* their efforts at caring for us. Back in the late 1980s I was teaching a Bible study. There were eighty-two people in that class. My wife's mother died suddenly and unexpectedly, and during the next three months, not a single one of those eighty-two people came to see us, brought food by, or called to check on us. We were stunned, and a depression began to set in. How could we be around so many people and call them friends; how could we be part of a church where this kind of thing happened among Christian brothers and sisters? As time passed, we eventually gathered some of those whom we thought were our closest leaders in the class and asked them what happened? Why did they not show they cared? Everyone, without exception, said the same thing. They said, "You two were our leaders, you always took care of *us*, so when it happened to you we didn't know what to do." It was not that they did not care; they just didn't know how to reach out to us, and we didn't recognize their distance as their inability to show they cared. Caring about others does not always come naturally; sometimes we have to learn how to care and how to show it.

So while we're talking about this, let me give you some tips for caring for someone who is hurting. When a person is hurting or depressed or going through a trial, do NOT ask, "What can I do to help?" That may seem totally counter-intuitive, but if you have ever been through a crisis, a depression, or a significant trial of any kind, you realize that someone asking what they can do to help you actually gives you one more decision to make when you already feel overwhelmed. You have to figure out what you can give them to do. So, the better approach, if you're trying to help is, don't ask. Do! In other words, it is better for you to do something you think will help than to place a burden on the person of finding something for you to do. You may not do the right thing, but the hurting person will eventually recognize that you are trying to show you care by doing what you did.

Let me give you an example. When someone goes through a death in his family, the world stops. Everything revolves around the family gathering, planning a memorial service, picking out a casket and gravesite, meeting with funeral homes or churches and pastors. But guess what, the yard still has to be mowed. Go mow their yard. Don't ask if you can, just do it. Their car will need to be clean for the meetings and family gatherings. Wash their car. They will need food at their house that is easy to prepare, without a lot of cooking. Go buy bread and sandwich meats, condiments and drinks and take them to the house. Don't ask, just do it. Now you have shown you care, and removed from them the burden of having to think of something for you to do.

Now let's look back at Isaiah 61. It says that God gives you something instead of the spirit of heaviness/depression. It says, "...*the mantle of praise instead of a spirit of fainting* (depression)." There is a *spirit* of depression. That spirit can come upon you and can torment you. It is a spirit that must be cast off of you. In the authority of Jesus' name, it must be commanded to leave you. It is real, and it is tragic, but it is under the authority that Jesus gives to us.

And listen, if you are depressed and hurting, you are not alone. The sky is not falling and you will survive this. There is always somebody who can one-up your tragedy. You will make it through. How do I know that? How do I know that you can survive a tragedy? You are sitting here reading this book. That means you have already survived some tough times. It means you have already made it through a tragedy. You're going to make it this time, too. Remember the last tough time? You are here now, so you made it past that one and you can do it again. If you doubt that, you need to understand that the core of depression is a misplaced belief. You are believing a reality for yourself that is not the truth.

What are the lies of depression?

That God does not have good plans for me.
That God's word is not the truth for me.
That I am not worthy of what God offers me.

Listen; I understand that in and of myself I am not worthy. But God tells me I am made worthy through Christ! The lie is, that whichever of these things I tell myself is more true than what God has to say. This may be hard to hear, but depression is actually a defiance of the promises of God. Just as Elijah thought he knew more about himself than God did, and raised his own opinion of himself above God's opinion, depression says, "I believe what I believe over what you have promised me, God." Depression is agreeing with the enemy about how things should go, and submitting to Satan's plans for your life.

So what do we do to avoid depression? In simple words, do not do what Elijah did. Do not run and hide. Do not isolate yourself. Do not listen to your own counsel. Do not try to convince God that you know you better than He knows you. Fight against the unscriptural feelings of depression – they are a warning sign of what is trying to take hold in you. Listen to your friends. If they are Christian, they will most likely be telling you the truth of God. Even if they don't know Christ, their counsel is better than yours right now. Either way, they are the ones in a clear place to think so they can give you sound advice.

And remember Proverbs 12:25 – *Anxiety in a man's heart weighs it down, but a good word makes it glad.*

This Scripture says that a good word makes the heart glad. On a physical level, a word can change everything. You have lost your job. The bills are stacking up, the stress of no income has set in, you do not know what the future holds and you are starting the process of lofty things and speculations. Then the phone rings. Someone you know found out you were out of a job and says, "Please come to work for me. I can pay you more than you were making at your old job." What happens to your heart? It becomes glad! The good word on the phone broke the heaviness.

Now think about that verse spiritually. Scripture says that life and death are in the power of the tongue, so you can speak life over your life or death over your life. Listen, depression is the tool of the enemy, and it shuts your mouth. Have you ever seen a chatty, depressed person? No one is the life of the party if they are depressed. When depression shuts the mouth, life cannot flow from the tongue because it has been silenced.

But if life is in the tongue and depression stops the tongue, how do you apply this truth spiritually? Don't believe the version of truth you've been telling yourself. Don't elevate Satan's lies above the Word of God. Defeat depression, the tool of the enemy, by *believing* God's truth, and *declaring* the truth that *He* gave you, rather than the one the enemy is offering.

Defeat the enemy by speaking the things of life – the mighty promises of God!

Five

Stronghold of Gossip

Some people don't think that gossip is a stronghold; they would say it's more of a sin. But a stronghold is a place the enemy hides something in your belief system. I want to tell you if you don't already know; gossip is full of lies – lies that are hidden well in that stronghold.

Now most pastors would simply refer you to the many verses in Scripture that talk about gossip. I could go to James 1, where it says to bridle your tongue. Or to Proverbs 6, where it says that the Lord hates those who spread strife. We could talk about the fact that in Romans 1, gossip is actually listed right up there with murder. It is also listed with greed, arrogance and deceit. I could use cliché' phrases like, "loose lips, sink ships." We could talk about how gossip breaks trust, and how it hurts people. But here is what will happen if I throw a bunch of verses at you about how gossip is bad – you will go into behavior modification and start saying you need to watch your mouth and control what you say. That would be like mowing a lawn that has weeds in it. When you are done mowing, everything looks level and good. But soon the weeds begin to outgrow the grass again, and the entire mess is right back where it started. Behavior modification does not solve the problem; it's time to pull the weeds.

Listen to me; gossip is like having a savage tiger in a cage. But having a savage tiger *in a cage* does not make it any less savage. What we want to do is change the heart; we want the cage empty and the tiger killed. We want freedom from these kinds of things. So, we have to look beyond behavior modification and simply controlling our tongue.

Here are three different definitions of gossip:

- Gossip, in English – A casual unconstrained conversation or reports about other people typically involving details that are not confirmed as being true

- Gossip, in Greek – *psithurismos* - Whispering

- Gossip, in Hebrew – *patha* – one who opens his lips

Gossip is not just saying negative things about someone. Gossip is talking about something that you cannot personally confirm is true. Basically, we are gossiping anytime we repeat something that is second-hand information. If we did not experience it, witness it, hear it or read it, or have first-hand knowledge of some kind, what we are saying is gossip because, in reality, we do not actually know if it is true. This becomes a real challenge. We are a culture that is very comfortable with repeating whatever we've heard. We like to "pass on" the story we heard about someone or something else. We like others to believe that we have information that they do not have, even if we cannot confirm the information we have is true. We feel free to do this because we can always say, "Well, that's what so and so told me," and this somehow relieves us of any accountability for what we said. This is a crisis in our nation today; one that we call "fake news." This is a situation where there is no confirmation of truth, but the freedom to declare whatever we want in order to make news.

When we gossip, it can reveal that we have a need to be placed above another person, and in order for that to happen we must demote that person. When we gossip, it can indicate that we have a need to be in the "know" so people will find us valuable. Gossip can reveal that you do not want reconciliation with others; you want or need retaliation, and you want it covertly. Gossip can be a way of trying to get vindication for something when you do not trust God to vindicate you.

Here's a curve ball. An accusation of gossip, when you did not hear the actual gossip, is gossip. What? Accusing someone of spreading gossip when you did not actually *hear* them gossiping, is gossip. You cannot confirm they were gossiping.

Ten lies the enemy plants in this stronghold:

- Gossip lies to us and tells us that we have something valuable to say.
- Gossip lies to us and tells us that others will think we have wisdom or insight that they do not have.
- Gossip lies to us and tells us that because we have this – information, we are important.
- Gossip lies to us and tells us our words will bond us closer to a friend if we share the gossip.
- Gossip lies to us and tells us that by sharing the gossip, our friends will be drawn to us and away from our foe.
- Gossip lies to us and tells us other people are not talking about us when we are talking about them (sowing and reaping.)
- Gossip lies to us and tells us no one will know we are saying bad things about him or her.

- Gossip lies to us and tells us we are defending a friend when what we are actually doing is spreading a rumor.
- Gossip lies to us and tells us that gossiping will not hurt our reputation.
- Gossip lies to us and tells us that we are not manipulating the situation or the person we are talking to when we gossip.

Think about that last lie. When we gossip, we want to manipulate a person or a situation. All gossip is connected to manipulation one way or another. Either you are trying to change a person's opinion about yourself, or their opinion about someone else.

The mature believer asks the question, "Why am I saying what I am saying?" Perhaps the more mature believer could adopt the catch phrase, "Pray it before you spray it." If I could pray it before I spray it, I might find out why I am saying it. It might help me to realize I am only talking to manipulate a situation. I am just talking to meet a need in me. I am just talking to get someone to change his opinion of someone else. Why do I think the person I am talking to needs the information I have?

Wise people know they do not know the whole story. Wise people know there are two sides to every story. Wise people know that there is always more to the story than what they are getting from one person. Wise people know how to wait until all the information is gathered before forming an opinion.

Wise people know if they speak based on someone else's information, they are setting a trap for themselves. Has this ever happened to you? Someone told you something that was gossip, you repeated it to others and then it turned about to be wrong or bad information. Who ended up looking bad? You.

Among the several connections to gossip in Scripture, these three are each a good indication of just how serious God considers this offense.

- Romans 1 – connects gossip with a depraved mind.
- Leviticus 19 – connects gossip with a murderous spirit.
- James 1:26 – connects gossip with spiritual worthlessness.

So here are four things to remember about gossip.

> - **Point one**. First and foremost, Gossip violates the Word of God! Remember that a thought can be set up against the Word of God and become a lofty thing. Then a lofty thing can become a speculation and eventually a stronghold. Gossip violates the Word of God!

Let's look at Psalm 5.

O Lord, lead me in Your righteousness because of my foes; Make Your way straight before me. There is nothing reliable in what they say; Their inward part is destruction itself. Their throat is an open grave; They flatter with their tongue. Hold them guilty, O God; By their own devices let them fall! In the multitude of their transgressions thrust them out, For they are rebellious against You.

(Psalm 5:8-10.)

Did you see that? *"There is nothing reliable in what they say."* That's gossip. Let them fall by their own devices for they are rebellious against you. Strong language for the words that come out of our mouths. Can you imagine the change in our lives if we recognized that the gossip we speak is not actually an offense against the person about whom we are speaking, but it is an offense against God? I will say it until the day I die; we will become a holy nation when we finally realize our accountability is not to others, it's to God!

Your tongue devises destruction, Like a sharp razor, O worker of deceit. (Psalm 52:2.)

- Point two – Gossip violates the reputation of the person we are speaking about! When we talk about someone else negatively, if we are successful in manipulating the opinion of the person we are talking to, then we have violated the reputation of the person who is the subject of that gossip.

For they have opened the wicked and deceitful mouth against me; They have spoken against me with a lying tongue. They have also surrounded me with words of hatred, And fought against me without cause.

(Psalm 109:2-3.)

LISTEN: Any time you repeat a story you heard, you are gossiping – speaking against someone – because you don't actually know if what you are saying is true. If you are hearing a story about someone and it is second hand, ask whoever is telling you to stop! Say to them, "I wasn't there. I do not need to know that." Even if it's coming from a friend you trust, you have to remember it is coming through your friend's filter of hurts and motivations. In other words, there is a reason your friend is telling you, and most likely it's to meet a need in themselves. They are trying to capture your friendship. They are trying to make you, or them, look better than the person they are gossiping about. Your friend may be trying to seem valuable because of the information they have.

> - **Point three** – Gossip violates the reputation of the person who is spreading it! Now we are talking about us. How does gossip reflect on us?

He who conceals hatred has lying lips, And he who spreads slander is a fool. When there are many words, transgression is unavoidable, But he who restrains his lips is wise.

(Proverbs 10:18-21.)

Always remember that when it comes to gossip, you will invariably be the one who eventually ends up looking bad. It will expose you. It will expose your character. You will lose your integrity.

> - **Point four** – Gossip affects the listener's impression. So now we are talking the person *receiving* the gossip. If you are the one listening, this means you.

Their tongue is a deadly arrow; It speaks deceit; With his mouth one speaks peace to his neighbor, But inwardly he sets an ambush for him.

(Jeremiah 9:8.)

The deceit that is being spoken is setting an ambush for the person hearing it. It may sound good. It may seem harmless, but it is a trap. If you are listening to gossip, you are being manipulated! Time after time after time I sit in my office and listen to people complain about what other people told them a third person said about them. So we call the third person up and ask if that is what they said. Inevitably, it is not and the situation is easily clarified. But when we go back to the gossiper their response is typically, "Well, that's what I *heard* they said about you." Do you see the trap? You are hurting the one you tell the gossip to. You are setting them up with bad information, and you are causing division where there was no division. Sounds just like a scheme of the enemy, doesn't it?

Gossip is a plan, it's a scheme; it's a covert operation by the enemy to cause hurt, chaos and division. Negative gossip cannot be of God. Why? Because you are not speaking truth, and God speaks only truth.

So what do we do about gossip? We have to recognize the opportunity to improve in this area, and the improvement plan starts with repentance. Some people think repentance is a scary word. But when you look at what the word really means, repentance actually becomes something we can desire. The Greek word, *metaneo,* means to change your mind. Now this is not like changing your mind about whether you want the steak or the chicken at a restaurant. This means a change of mind that changes you. This is a change of mind that changes your belief system. And when your belief system changes, your soul responds to that new belief. We become transformed by the renewing of our mind. Our mind takes a new path that transforms our actions. If there is no change in our behavior, then there was no repentance. The evidence of repentance is a change in how we act.

Next, we need to fight for unity. Do not allow the enemy to bring disunity into the family of God! When Akin went into

Jericho with disunity, it caused the Israelite nation to lose the battle and thirty-six men at Ai. Just one man decided he would not come into unity with the rest of the children of God and it cost them all dearly. Unity is a major goal within the Christian faith.

Pray for spiritual eyes and ears. We need to clearly discern what is going on in the spirit around us. When the devil is at work, we should sense it. We should be able to feel that something is not right in our spirit. Evil is present, a plan is at work against us. We need to pray to be able to see in the spirit as well, if not better, than we do in the physical. The Kingdom of God is spiritual.

Confront. Confront in love. We are called to strengthen each other. We are called to lovingly rebuke one another. We are called to fight for unity among the church at large, and *that* unity can come only with occasional confrontation between believers. But I have found the best way to handle that confrontation is by us believing the best about each other. We will have a completely different conversation if I come to you in disbelief that you could have done this thing, rather than coming at you with an accusation that you did something wrong. If we were to start the confrontations believing that the other person had only good intentions instead of bringing our hurt and accusations in first, we might be more willing to hear that there was no malicious intent in the first place.

As believers, we must put all our cards on the table. No more listening to what someone else said without that person there. No more settling problems without all the players present. No more accusations without first-hand knowledge. No more decisions based on the data of only one side of the story.

We must stop thinking that we are always right about whatever we have believed. Guess what, you might be wrong. But some hurt inside you is going to want you to press in, in order to protect yourself. It will make you want to constantly stand your ground so you do not have to admit that you were wrong. But maybe you *are* wrong. What would happen if we were humble enough to accept from the beginning that we might be wrong? Would it allow us to keep our mouths shut and wait for the truth, instead of blurting out the gossip we received?

Also remember, the fact that you have an opinion does not necessarily mean you need to express it. Wisdom will dictate that there are times when your opinion may not have value to resolving the problem. You've heard it said before that it is better to keep your mouth shut and let everyone think you are a fool, then to open your mouth and prove you are.

Fighting gossip is a spiritual battle and we must see it as one. We are not each other's enemy. But Satan is God's enemy, so he tries to use our words to each other to steal, kill and destroy, and to keep us from the Kingdom of God.

Gossip is an offense against God, and violates the word of God. But remember that savage tiger? Gossip is not the only dangerous way in which we can use our tongues. For all the reasons we've already discussed here – our hurts, our needs, our desire to be liked and accepted – we can let that tiger loose even when we simply use the truth unwisely, or twist the truth to manipulate a situation, and certainly when we out and out lie to illicit a particular outcome. There can be dangerous power in our tongues. But even *knowing* that the power of death and life are in the tongue, it can be a real challenge for us sometimes to truly think about what we are saying and why we are saying it. Considering how much damage and chaos our words can create in our lives and the lives of the people around us, the next time Satan tries to create that chaos and division within us, perhaps we, as believers, need to try something new; to stop – and say, "WAIT."

So let's talk for a moment about that. In this context, I'm not using WAIT to mean "delay", "hold for a moment," or "be patient," but rather WAIT as an acronym for Why Am I Talking? This is the question we should ask. If we were to stop in the middle of most of our conversations and genuinely ask ourselves, "Why am I even saying the things I am saying?" we would eliminate a tremendous amount of gossip and lies and unhealthy speech from our lives.

If we do *not* stop and say WAIT, Satan can and will tempt us to use our tongues in order to create division. And this scheme of the devil can bite you back! I am not suggesting that we don't talk to each other. I am saying that we need to begin to consider what is coming out of our mouths and determine whether it is death or life – because if we don't, we could be opening the door to Satan and falling right into his plan to cause upheaval and turmoil in our lives. Remember, Satan is the father of all lies, and he delights in using them against us to create chaos.

We know that death and life are in the power of the tongue, so *every word we speak is important!*

Genesis 39 is a story about Joseph. We are pretty familiar with his story. Joseph is sold into slavery by his brothers, who then lie to their father about what happened to Joseph. After rising to power in Egypt in Potiphar's house, Joseph is falsely accused of trying to seduce Potiphar's wife. He then spends several years in jail before returning to power after interpreting a dream.

> *Now it happened one day that he went into the house to do his work, and none of the men of the household was there inside. She caught him by his garment, saying, "Lie with me!" And he left his garment in her hand and fled, and went outside. When she saw that he had left his garment in her hand and had fled outside, she called to the men of her household and said to them, "See, he has brought in a Hebrew to us to make sport of us; he came in to me to lie with me, and I screamed. When he heard that I raised my voice and screamed, he left his garment beside me and fled and went outside." So she left his garment beside her until his master came home. Then she spoke to him with these words, "The Hebrew slave, whom you brought to us, came in to me to make sport of me; and as I raised my voice and screamed, he left his garment beside me and fled outside." Now when his master heard the words of his wife, which she spoke to him, saying, "This is what your slave did to me," his anger burned. So Joseph's master took him and put him into the jail, the place where the king's prisoners were confined; and he was there in the jail.*
>
> (Genesis 39:11-20).

Here is the question we want to answer: Why is this happening to Joseph? The master received some second-hand information (a bad report), from his wife, believed it and Joseph ends up in jail. You might say that this is all part of the grand scheme of God for the redemption and salvation of Joseph's family one day. And you might say God was using this situation to set things up for the great reunion and reconciliation of Joseph and his brothers. You might even say that this is all part of how God works all things together for good for those who love Him and are called to His purposes. And I would say all of that could be true. However, there is another God principle at work here.

Let's go back to Genesis 37.

Now Jacob lived in the land where his father had sojourned, in the land of Canaan. These are the records of the generations of Jacob. Joseph, when seventeen years of age, was pasturing the flock with his brothers while he was still a youth, along with the sons of Bilhah and the sons of Zilpah, his father's wives. And Joseph brought back a bad report about them to their father."

(Genesis 37:1-2.)

Did you notice it said that Joseph brought back a *bad* report about his brothers to Jacob? When I first read this I assumed that his brothers must have been doing something bad, and that Joseph had gone back and told his father about whatever that bad thing was. But when you look at the word used for "bad report" in Hebrew, the word is *dibbah*. This word means an evil or defamatory report. In other words, the report itself was corrupt. It was an evil report, not a report about evil being done by his brothers. Joseph was bringing to his father an untrue report, a lie, to make his brothers look bad. That was the source of Potiphar's wife bringing an untrue, evil report about Joseph to Potiphar. It is the biblical concept of sowing and reaping. Joseph had sown a "dibbah" report and was now *reaping* a "dibbah" report from Potiphar's wife.

While we are on the topic of sowing and reaping, most teachers will warn you to watch what you are sowing because one day you will reap that very same thing. But today, I want to ask you to do something different. I want you to consider what you are currently reaping. What is going on in your life today? Are your finances good? Are your friendships good? Are people criticizing you? Are there people who do not trust you? When you can establish what you are reaping right now in your life, then you can easily determine what you have sown in the past. That can either be a very painful or satisfying evaluation. But if you believe in the biblical principle of sowing and reaping, then whatever you are reaping now, you sowed in the past. Because you have already experienced the reaping, when you complete this exercise, you will more clearly see what you want to change about your sowing now and in the future.

So when it comes to gossip, we see by the definitions that it does not always have to be a negative report; it could simply be a report that you cannot confirm yourself. However, there are also times when you just need to keep what you know to yourself. In other words, just because you know something does not necessarily mean you need to share it.

Remember that the precursor to these next verses is that Joseph had given a bad (evil or defamatory) report about his brothers.

Then Joseph had a dream, and when he told it to his brothers, they hated him even more. He said to them, "Please listen to this dream which I have had; for behold, we were binding sheaves in the field, and lo, my sheaf rose up and also stood erect; and behold, your sheaves gathered around and bowed down to my sheaf." Then his brothers said to him, *"Are you actually going to reign over us? Or are you really going to rule over us?"* So, they hated him even more for his dreams and for his words.

(Genesis 37:5-8.)

Now, is it the truth that Joseph had this dream? Yes. What happens when he tells his brothers his dream? They hate him even more. But it doesn't stop there:

Now he had still another dream, and related it to his brothers, and said, "Lo, I have had still another dream; and behold, the sun and the moon and eleven stars were bowing down to me." He related it to his father and to his brothers; and his father rebuked him and said to him, "What is this dream that you have had? Shall I and your mother and your brothers actually come to bow ourselves down before you to the ground?"

(Genesis 37:9-10.)

It is true that Joseph had these dreams so let me ask a few more questions. Are these prophetic dreams? Yes. We know this by reading on in the book of Genesis. Does Joseph have first-hand knowledge of the dreams? Yes, they were his personal dreams. But, does he need to tell both of the dreams to his family when they are already angry with him? Are not both of the dreams on the same subject? What if he had held onto the first one and told them only the second one? I am not saying God does not have a purpose in all this, but what I am saying is that maybe it would have been wiser for Joseph to ask the question, "Why Am I Talking?" before opening his lips. It might have prevented a lot of trouble for his family.

These stories about Joseph are not examples of gossip based on the typical understanding of the word, or the English definition of gossip. But remember the definition stated above from the Hebrew – *patha* – is "one who opens his lips." There are other people in the Bible that spoke the truth as well, but then wished that they had not. Samson, for example. He eventually tells Delilah the truth, but it costs him his eyesight and his freedom. Perhaps there should be times when we know the truth, but are wise enough not to speak it out. Clearly both Joseph and Samson suffered because they opened their lips and did not say WAIT.

Most of the time the reason we are talking about someone else, is that we are actually trying to meet a need in us. *Ouch.* We have a need to feel better about ourselves. We have a need to elevate ourselves above someone else. We have a need to expose them. We have a need to feel valuable because of the information we have. Or maybe we just need to feel closer to a friend and we believe the information we have will help that person like us more.

The good man out of the good treasure of his heart brings forth what is good; and the evil man out of the evil treasure brings forth that which is evil; for his mouth speaks from that which fills his heart.

(Luke 6:45.)

In the final analysis, it's the condition of our heart that dictates whether or not we gossip and how we use the power of our tongues in general. We can be operating from a place that is full of hurts and needs and lies – one that drives us to say

80

things that should not be said – without us even knowing we are in that place. So it might be worth considering; do you have a stronghold? Do you have a savage tiger in a cage? It takes a period of honest evaluation to determine the answer to that. I would encourage you to designate a time frame – perhaps a week or a month – during which you evaluate each conversation you have to see. Ask yourself, "Did I gossip? Did I manipulate someone or something with my words? Did I need to say what I said, or did I say it to fulfill some need in me? It can be a tough analysis to make, but the question should always be, "How am I using the power of my tongue? Am I speaking life or am I speaking death?" If it isn't life, then WAIT!

Six

Stronghold of Sexual Lust

The stronghold of sexual lust is host to the spirit of lust, which brings a number of deceptions and lies into our lives.

One lie, for example, is that pornography does not hurt anyone. Another is that fornication is okay as long as both people involved agree to it. And a third is that if my sexual needs are not being met within my marriage, it is acceptable to go outside the marriage to have them met.

Satan is hiding in each of these beliefs, so in order to expose him and the lies for what they really are, let's start with some definitions.

- Pornography: Any sexually explicit or sexually arousing material. It can be different for different people, but you will know what it is for you.

- Fornication: Sexual activity outside of marriage. Straight, gay or bi-sexual, it does not matter. If it is outside of marriage, it is fornication. And let's be sure to include *any* sexual activity, not just intercourse.

- Adultery: Going outside of the marriage relationship for *any* sexual activity. Here too, straight, gay or bi-sexual, it does not matter. If you are married and you go outside of that covenant for sex, it is adultery.

All three of these are related to the spirit of lust in Scripture. We want to look at how the spirit of lust operates so if it comes against you, you can see it and stop its progress at the thought level. Lust is something that affects every human being at some time and at some level in our lives. Because it is a spirit, it has a scheme to overtake you. Therefore, we have to be wise and learn how it operates in order to expose its plan.

To study the spirit of lust we need to go to Proverbs chapter 7. In this chapter, a physical story is portrayed so that we can learn about a spiritual issue. We will go through the entire Proverb in order to understand how this spirit works, and how we can detect it. This story is the physical story of how a woman seduces a man, but spiritually it represents how the spirit of lust operates.

Proverbs 7:1 says, *"My son, keep my words And treasure my commandments within you."*

To get us off on the right track in relaying this story, the Scripture starts by calling you "son." The obvious implication here is that we are going to be getting advice from a father. The father speaking to you here is God.

Keep my commandments and live,
And my teaching as the apple of your eye.

God begins by giving us a very basic principle; life comes by keeping the commandments of God. So many people look at the Bible as the rulebook of God, but that was never what He intended. The Bible is a plan for life, joy, peace, abundance and relationship. Through keeping the commandments of God, we will see life – life as God planned it to be. Here He tells us to keep our eyes on His teachings and we will *experience* that life. If we choose to not follow the teachings of God, as Adam and Eve did, we will experience death biblically – a separation from God. How different their lives would have been if Adam and Eve had kept their eyes on His teachings, rather than on the fruit of that tree.

Bind them on your fingers;
Write them on the tablet of your heart.

I believe this verse speaks to two different applications. First, binding it on our fingers means to put it into practice. The hands represent doing something. To have His teachings bound to our fingers means that whatever we put our hands to is in line with what He has taught us. To write them on the tablet of our hearts speaks to having them memorized and ingrained in our very soul.

Say to wisdom, "You are my sister,"
And call understanding your intimate friend;

In other words, when you are having a conversation with wisdom, when you are engaged with wisdom, when you are hearing from wisdom, say, "You are my sister." This speaks to the desire to have a close, bonded relationship with wisdom. He is speaking about making sure that you hold wisdom as close as you hold family. He then goes on to say that "understanding" has to be an intimate friend. This is taking it a step further, past just family now, and is talking about someone that you know inside and out. And in order to have this kind of intimate understanding, we need to pursue the knowledge of something on more than just a surface level.

That they may keep you from an adulteress,

From the foreigner who flatters with her words.

In the next verse, we identify the spirit of lust. God has given us the instruction that we must pursue His commandments and His teachings, to get wisdom and understanding for the purpose of keeping us from the adulteress. By the words He's using, you can see that the adulteress must be a cunning and sly foe, and that we have to be intimately acquainted with wisdom in order to keep ourselves from her.

> *For at the window of my house*
> *I looked out through my lattice,*
> *And I saw among the naive,*
> *And discerned among the youths*
> *A young man lacking sense,*

Solomon was looking out through the lattice and could see a young man who lacked sense. Solomon is saying here that it was so obvious you could see it all over the young man! He knew that this young man was headed for trouble and did not have the wisdom and understanding to prevent what was about to happen to him.

So, at this point, let's start making a list of Hide and Seek lessons we can learn from exploring this chapter and the spirit of lust.

> - Lesson 1. Do not be naïve about the spirit of lust – have wisdom and understanding.

Passing through the street near her corner;

Because he was naïve, he was traveling near the corner that

led to her house. He was in the vicinity. He wasn't there yet, but he was close. He hadn't committed to it, but he was considering it. Do you know what it feels like to be right on the boarder of falling into temptation? We have not made the critical leap yet, but we are considering it, coming close, thinking hard about giving in to it.

- You know that some computer privacy is available.

- You know that he or she is soon going to be coming by your office.

- You know that you could respond to their text in an inappropriate way if you wanted to be just a little bit playful.

- Lesson 2. DO NOT GO NEAR IT!

Now flee from youthful lusts and pursue righteousness, faith, love and peace, with those who call on the Lord from a pure heart.

(2 Timothy 2:22.)

This is the *only* time in Scripture that God tells us to run away. Interesting, the only time a Christian needs to high tail it and get out of there is when the spirit of lust is in the vicinity. God does not say, "Use your authority against it." He does not say, "Command that thing to leave." He does not say, "Stand," like He does in Ephesians 6. No, here He tells us to *run away!* Not just leave, but flee! Not only that, He tells us *where* to run. He says that when you run away from lust, run *to* righteousness, faith, love and peace with those who call on the Lord from a pure heart. Here is what He is saying: If you see lust coming, turn to righteousness. Turn to those you know know the Lord. Turn to faith. There is no ambiguity as to which way you are going once you realize you are on the verge of making a bad decision, because anything past this point that is *not* running away is moving *toward* the mistake. And any move toward lust is a move away from righteousness. You are on the precipice of leaving faith, love and peace, and headed toward disaster. So let's see what this naïve young man does:

.... And he takes the way to her house,

Boom! He just took the bait. It's when you say, okay, a few minutes of porn. It's when you reach your hand out to someone you are not married to. It's when you decide to send that flirtatious text or that inappropriate picture. I remember hearing the story of a minister who was caught up in an affair. As he explained how it happened, he said he knew the exact moment when he crossed the line into adultery. He had been counseling a woman for several sessions. One day while they were alone, she was telling him that her husband treated her poorly. His response was, "If I were your husband, I would never treat you that way." Then he said, "When I heard those words roll off my lips and saw how they hit her, I knew we had just crossed over into a place that would end up with us in a bed."

But put on the Lord Jesus Christ and make no provision for the flesh in regard to its lust.
                                            (Romans 13:14.)

Make no provision for lust. Make no plans that would include lust. Do not take the path to its house.

In the twilight, in the evening,
In the middle of the night and in the darkness.

This is a very interesting Scripture in this story. He goes to her house in the nighttime, under the cover of darkness. If you remember the story of David and Bathsheba, David thought things could be done in secret. There is a reason that the spirit of lust wants to make you think that. It's because we fail to believe that our sins will be found out. We think, "What's the harm?" if no one knows. This is where we must take on the attitude that our accountability is never to man; it is to God. Whether or not other people know what I did is unimportant compared to the fact that God sees all that is done in the dark.

And behold, a woman comes to meet him,
dressed as a harlot and cunning of heart.

The spirit of lust will present herself in an alluring way. The spirit of lust will actually *come after* you with its lies and deceit. The spirit of lust will pursue you with a cunning plan; it will draw you in. And she knows when you take the bait.

She is boisterous and rebellious,
Her feet do not remain at home;
She is now in the streets, now in the squares,
And lurks by every corner.

The spirit of lust is intentional. She is a cunning predator that hides herself in the open and lurks by every corner, ready to leap out and grab you. The spirit of lust knows what she is doing, and you have to recognize that it has a plan in order to fight her.

> - Lesson 4. Know that the spirit of lust will try to incorporate God in its deception, because it knows God is of value to you.

So she seizes him and kisses him
And with a brazen face she says to him:
"I was due to offer peace offerings;
Today I have paid my vows."

What is a peace offering? A peace offering under Levitical law is the most unique of all the offerings. For a peace offering, you brought the choicest meat to the temple for sacrifice, but you did not leave it there; you took it back home with you to eat that day. So what is the spirit of lust saying here? "I have already been to church and I am right with God, so let's eat this offering of choice meat together." This is stunning! The spirit of lust is cunning and will try to bring God into your adulterous relationship! When it comes to porn, the spirit of lust will say, "Don't worry, God understands and will forgive you." In fornication, the spirit of lust will say, "But we love each other and God knows we want to be together forever." In adultery, the spirit of lust will say, "You married the wrong person and they have kept you from your real calling in God."

This is why there are so many affairs in the church. The spirit of lust will bring God into the picture in a way that allows you to stay in touch with God while stepping into the lustful relationship. Lust knows that if it can incorporate God, you will more easily fall.

I know people in adultery and fornication situations that say, "We pray together," or "We have Bible studies together." But we must always remember that as Christians, we are the chosen, to be the bride of Christ. When you step out of the covenant bride relationship with Christ in the Kingdom of God, and step into the enemy's camp in the kingdom of darkness, you are committing adultery against the Kingdom of God and Jesus, your groom. Praying together or having bible studies together does not change that. I don't say this to bring condemnation over you, but to make it clear why, in Scripture, God takes adultery so seriously. It is a marriage covenant breaker.

> - Lesson 5. The spirit of lust wants you to need, and feel needed by her.

Therefore I have come out to meet you, To seek your presence earnestly, and I have found you.

This is the spirit of lust speaking. She's saying, "I need you," "We can meet each other's needs," "We are good for each other and I'm glad I found you." The spirit of lust will convince you that you have answered her deep desire to find you.

I have spread my couch with coverings, With colored linens of Egypt.

I have sprinkled my bed
With myrrh, aloes and cinnamon.
Come, let us drink our fill of love until morning;
Let us delight ourselves with caresses.

The spirit of lust will woo you. She will entice you with things that appeal to you and make you believe you'll have an experience like never before. How does that play out? In pornography she says, "I will show you something even more enticing and erotic than you've seen before." In fornication, "You made me feel so wonderful, surely we can go even further together." In adultery, "Let me give you something you are not getting at home in your marriage.

- Lesson 6. The spirit of lust will make you feel safe.

For my husband is not at home,
He has gone on a long journey;
He has taken a bag of money with him,
At the full moon he will come home.

The spirit of lust is saying, "My husband is gone. I know where he has gone, how long he will be gone and when he will be home." The deception of the spirit of lust here is that she will keep you safe from being exposed. This is different from just the lie that what you're doing can be done in secret. It adds the element of time to the secrecy factor. It says, "You and I have a window of time during which we can safely be together, so you can relax and enjoy.

- Lesson 7. The spirit of lust will lie to you and tell you what you need to hear.

With her many persuasions she entices him;
With her flattering lips she seduces him.

In pornography, the spirit of lust will say you are not hurting anyone. In fornication, it will say that everything we do is okay because we're in love. In adultery, it will tell us she will be there to meet our needs because our spouse is not.

> - Lesson 8. You will suffer, you will be in bondage, and it will bring death into your life.

Now the Scripture takes us in a different direction. The spirit of lust has already succeeded in her enticement and we will learn about the fruit of this relationship.

Suddenly he follows her
As an ox goes to the slaughter,

This is a very accurate depiction when you look at the process of slaughtering animals. The animals walk freely into the slaughterhouse because the farmer doesn't indicate to the animals that they are about to be slaughtered. They go in completely unwittingly; the cows have no idea what is coming.

Or as one in fetters to the discipline of a fool,
Until an arrow pierces through his liver;
As a bird hastens to the snare,
So he does not know that it will cost him his life.

He does not know it will cost him his life. That is not only profound, but an absolute truth. The spirit of lust can make you blind. It's part of her cunningness, her deceit. The spirit of lust desires to chain you, to pierce you, to snare you and to slaughter you.

When I counsel people who are going to get married, I tell them, "If you chose to get involved in sexual activity before you are married, expect the consequences to be sexual difficulties when you are married." There is a sowing and reaping principle with God. If you sow into sexual sin, you will reap sexual difficulties. You cannot abuse sex when you are single and not expect sexual consequences.

Now, in the Scripture, the father tells us what to do since the spirit of lust is out there lurking, waiting to capture us.

> *Now therefore, my sons, listen to me,*
> *And pay attention to the words of my mouth.*
> *Do not let your heart turn aside to her ways,*
> *Do not stray into her paths.*
> *For many are the victims she has cast down,*
> *And numerous are all her slain.*
> *Her house is the way to Sheol,*
> *Descending to the chambers of death.*

The father is saying, "LISTEN TO ME!" Stay away! Danger, danger, danger, Will Robinson! Do not go there! This road leads to death!

Many people today have an addiction to pornography. It is truly a difficult thing to escape. There is guilt and shame involved, and yet a constant returning to something you do not want to do. But look at this Scripture:

> *For the mind set on the flesh is death, but the mind set*
> *on the Spirit is life and peace because the mind set on*
> *the flesh is hostile toward God; for it does not subject*
> *itself to the law of God, for it is not even able to do so*

and those who are in the flesh cannot please God.
However, you are not in the flesh but in the Spirit if
God dwells in you. But if anyone does not have the
Spirit of Christ, he does not belong to Him.

(Romans 8:6-9.)

What I'm about to say may seem harsh, but hear me out. If you are struggling with pornography, fornication or adultery and there is no guilt, shame or remorse, you may need to check to see if Christ is in you. Here is why I say that. When we come to know Christ, our spirit is brought to life and the Holy Spirit comes to dwell within us. So we have entered the Kingdom of God and His very Spirit makes us a temple of the living God. If the Spirit of God dwells in us, can we look at pornography or go into the bed of adultery or fornication without creating a conflict within ourselves? Would not holiness and sinfulness be at war within us? I'm not saying that we are perfect people, but part of the sanctification process is being convicted by sin. If that conviction does not exist, then perhaps there is nothing within us that is in conflict with the sin. I am not speaking of condemnation. I am speaking of conviction. Condemnation says, "I am bad." Conviction says, "I am better than this." Condemnation is from the enemy and is used to make me feel bad about me. Conviction is from the Holy Spirit and reminds me I can overcome this.

If Christ is in you, though the body is dead because of
sin, yet the spirit is alive because of righteousness. But
if the Spirit of Him who raised Jesus from the dead
dwells in you, He who raised Christ Jesus from the
dead will also give life to your mortal bodies through
His Spirit who dwells in you. So then, brethren, we are
under obligation, not to the flesh, to live according to

the flesh—for if you are living according to the flesh, you must die; but if by the Spirit you are putting to death the deeds of the body, you will live.

(Romans 8:10-13.)

Notice what Romans 8:10-13 says. If you're living by the Spirit you are putting to death the deeds of the body. In other words, if you are living by the Spirit, the *deeds* of the body (the things you are doing *in* the body) are being put to death so you can live.

So how do we stop the spirit of lust at the thought level, so it doesn't move on to lofty things, speculations, or the ultimate stronghold? When I talk to men about pornography, fornication and adultery, I ask them to ask themselves the following questions:

- On these subjects, (pornography, fornication an adultery) how would you counsel your son or daughter?
- If God is a father, what does He think as *your* father, of what you are doing?
- What is your justification for what you are doing? Is that justification anything other than selfish?
- How long will the images and activities stay in your memory? (40 years later I can still remember what I saw in a pornographic movie I watched as a teenager.)
- What do you think about a guy who hides at his computer in the middle of the night to look at porn?
- When you explain this to your future spouse, how will it make them feel about you?

To be blunt, you cannot worship Jesus while you're looking at porn. You cannot worship Jesus while sleeping with someone you are not married to. You cannot worship Jesus while having an adulterous affair.

I, the Lord, search the heart, I test the mind, even to give to each man according to his ways, according to the results of his deeds. (Jeremiah 17:10.)

I think the actions that we are involved in reveal our hearts. And there are things within us that are being measured, so that the appropriate reward/consequence can be given to us.

Look at the scripture where Paul talks about what it means to be unrepentant of immorality.

I am afraid that when I come again my God may humiliate me before you, and I may mourn over many of those who have sinned in the past and not repented of the impurity, immorality and sensuality which they have practiced.
(2 Corinthians 12:21.)

Lust is not a new problem; it has been around for thousands of years. Paul is saying that it will grieve him greatly if the Corinthians do not turn away from the sins of their past. And it is no mistake that he lists impurity, immorality, and sensuality as the sins concerning him.

Second Corinthians 7:10 says, *"For the sorrow that is according to the will of God produces a repentance without regret, leading to salvation, but the sorrow of the world produces death."*

Lets dig into this. There are two categories here: the sorrow that is according to the will of God and the sorrow of the world. The sorrow of the world is, "I don't want consequences for my actions. I don't want the consequence of death that this decision brings. I feel bad because I got caught. I feel bad because I am no longer trusted. I feel bad because I hurt you; I regret what I did." These things represent the sorrow of the world.

But there is another kind of sorrow, the sorrow that recognizes I have offended God. It is a sorrow that recognizes the will of God. In other words, I am sorry because I have gone outside of the will of God for my life. I am sorry because I have not heeded the words of God for my life. This sorrow, which is directed toward my offense to God, produces repentance in me without regret. Why? Because, when I have repentance towards God, regret is removed. God puts my offense as far as the east is from the west. It is remembered no more.

Listen, when you hold yourself accountable to the world, there is always a way out for you. People can and should have others who can help hold them accountable to the Christian walk. But... you can lie, you can hide, you can conceal truth from other people. There is no human accountability, no accountability in this world that is valid. The only valid accountability is to God. And when we use God as our accountability we will repent, because we cannot hide and we cannot lie before Him!

Are you willing to repent because you have offended God with your sexual sin? Or do you still think you should be forgiven, and not have to suffer the earthly consequences of allowing the stronghold of lust to invade your life? Sex is a sacred gift that God gave to men and women in the union of marriage. Any use outside of that union is not in His plan, and is an offense to God.

When we expose the lies and deceptions that created the stronghold of lust in the first place, we can then repent before God for our misuse of what He made sacred. And with that repentance comes a forgiveness, that allows us to walk forward without regrets, and our sins are remembered no more.

Seven

Stronghold of Victimization

Let's start this discussion by asking a few questions. Are you suffering because of something someone else did or said to you? If I were to ask you, could you tell me with vivid detail what happened and how you got hurt? Do you believe that things are not working in your favor at this point in your life? Do you believe that there is nothing you can do about the problem you're facing, or the things that happened to you are not your fault? If you do, you are not alone. But you are believing Satan's lies.

What does it mean to have a stronghold of victimization? Most people don't even recognize that they are in a stronghold of victimization. But let's go the Bible and see where the first example of victimization is in Scripture. It doesn't take long as we look at Genesis, chapter 3. Adam and Eve are in the garden and have been told not to eat from a particular tree there. However, Satan comes along and deceives them into doing just the opposite.

And He (God) *said, "Who told you that you were naked? Have you eaten from the tree of which I commanded you not to eat?" The man said, "The woman whom You gave to be with me, she gave me from the tree, and I ate."*

(Genesis 3:11-12.)

Notice what Adam says – It's the woman's fault. And it's your fault, God, for giving me the woman. I have already eaten, so there is nothing I can do about it now, and I am not going to take any responsibility for having disobeyed you. I am the victim here.

There is another prime example in Scripture of the victim mentality. Saul is ruling over the Israelite nation and they are about to do battle with the Philistines. Saul is instructed to wait, before the Israelites go into battle, until Samuel has come to offer sacrifices for them.

> *Now he waited seven days, according to the appointed time set by Samuel, but Samuel did not come to Gilgal; and the people were scattering from him. So Saul said, "Bring to me the burnt offering and the peace offerings." And he offered the burnt offering. As soon as he finished offering the burnt offering, behold, Samuel came; and Saul went out to meet him and to greet him. But Samuel said, "What have you done?" And Saul said, "Because I saw that the people were scattering from me, and that you did not come within the appointed days, and that the Philistines were assembling at Michmash, therefore I said, 'Now the Philistines will come down against me at Gilgal, and I have not asked the favor of the Lord.' So I forced myself and offered the burnt offering"*
>
> (1 Samuel 13:8.)

Notice what Saul says – It is the people's fault. And it is your fault, Samuel, for not coming. It is the enemy's fault for assembling against me. Then Saul says, "I forced myself and offered the burnt offering." In other words, I was in such a bad way with the people – you did not come to my aid when you were supposed to and the enemy was obviously out to get me – so I forced myself to do something I was not supposed to do. You can see how Saul is not going to take responsibility for making the sacrifice that he was told Samuel was supposed to make. Saul considers himself the victim in the situation.

Now let's look at the results of Saul's decision.

Samuel said to Saul, "You have acted foolishly; you have not kept the commandment of the Lord your God, which He commanded you, for now the Lord would have established your kingdom over Israel forever. But now your kingdom shall not endure. The Lord has sought out for Himself a man after His own heart, and the Lord has appointed him as ruler over His people, because you have not kept what the Lord commanded you."

(1Samuel 13:13-14.)

Saul will now lose his kingdom and God will give it to David, because Saul has acted foolishly and shows no repentance for his own actions. The stronghold of victimization makes us not want to take responsibility for ourselves; we need to blame someone else and, finally, we need everyone to *see* us as the victim.

It's a hard thing to address because there are real hurts, real pains, real struggles that we all have to deal with. But the question is, how do we react to these occurrences? We begin to allow ourselves to take on this victim mentality and it becomes so prevalent in our lives that it is acceptable and even applauded. This victim mentality invades even the church.

In Exodus 14, the Israelite nation has been delivered from slavery out of Egypt. They have literally walked out of that slavery and begun their journey to the Promised Land. But now, crossing the Negev and soon to enter their promised destination, they are being chased down by Pharaoh who is not happy about their departure. The people have their freedom and their God, but something is happening among them.

As Pharaoh drew near, the sons of Israel looked, and behold, the Egyptians were marching after them, and they became very frightened; so the sons of Israel cried out to the Lord. Then they said to Moses, "Is it because there were no graves in Egypt that you have taken us away to die in the wilderness? Why have you dealt with us in this way, bringing us out of Egypt? Is this not the word that we spoke to you in Egypt, saying, 'Leave us alone that we may serve the Egyptians'? For it would have been better for us to serve the Egyptians than to die in the wilderness."

(Exodus 14:10-12.)

That last statement is a very interesting one. We know that every first-born of Egypt died the night they departed. That was an astronomical number of deaths and required an equal number of graves. In other words, Egypt was overburdened with graves for the dead. There were no places for graves left in Egypt, so the people are asking if this was why Moses brought them out to the desert to die. They then go so far as to say it would be better to be back in Egypt as slaves than to be there in the wilderness in freedom!

Here is the actual problem with the Israelites at that time. The Israelites had come out of Egypt, but Egypt had not come out of the Israelites. They were continuing to act as though they were still slaves because they had a slave mentality. They may have physically left their slavery, but in their minds they were slaves, still, so their response mirrored that mentality; they would be better off with what they knew – living as victims (slaves) – than they would be having their freedom. But let's not forget that when they left Egypt they walked out with the plunder of Egypt's gold and silver. They were wealthy people, on their way to a new land that God had promised them, but they could not see past their current condition to assess their real situation. They were free, they were in charge of their own destiny, they could pick their leaders and they could chart their own path, but they would rather return to their slavery.

It's actually kind of humorous when you think about it. Here are six hundred thousand men, their wives and families; so probably no fewer than two million people. Picture Moses, with his back to Egypt, facing the two million people and telling them they can't return! Can you see them groveling, looking at the ground and saying, "Oh man, Moses isn't going to let us go back to Egypt so I guess we have to stay out here?" Seriously? Is it not obvious that if they'd really wanted to go back they could easily have revolted and returned? You see, not being allowed to go back to Egypt wasn't the problem. The problem was that they considered themselves victims. They wanted only to whine, and not take any responsibility for doing something about their situation. They did not have a desire to return to Egypt; they had a desire to be victims, to blame someone else, and claim they could do nothing about it.

Listen, in order for you to be a victim you have to bring

your past into your present. To be a victim you have to allow your past hurt to prevent your future success. Victims stop the process of growing, allowing their past hurts to dominate their current life.

Do you know why the rearview mirror in your car is so small and the windshield is so big? It is because what is behind you is insignificant compared to what is ahead of you! And you will never move into your destiny until you leave your history!

I need to make a disclaimer here. I am going to use a Scripture out of context, but I am using it so that you grasp a thought, not understand a doctrine. What is spoken of in this Scripture is not victimization, but the concept is true, and valid in this discussion as well. The Scripture is 1 Corinthians 13, and Paul is addressing spiritual gifts. He is explaining that the gifts are here only until Christ returns, but once Christ returns we will not need the gifts.

When I was a child, I used to speak like a child, think like a child, reason like a child; when I became a man, I did away with childish things.
(1 Corinthians 13:11.)

What Paul is saying here is that in order for us to grow up, we have to put away childish things. What are childish things? They are the things of our past. They are the things that are behind us, not ahead of us. No one grows up *into* childish things. There are thought processes that we put behind us in order to move forward in our growing up process. And notice specifically Paul says here that he *makes the decision* to do away with childish things. He intentionally looks at the things of his past and does away with them. They are not going to help his future. They are not going to help his growing up. They are not going to help his destiny, so he has to "do away" with them. Paul says, "I did away with them because they are holding me to the past, and I need to move forward."

So here is where it gets a little tough. There are people who spend years defending a divorce. There are people who spend years mourning a death. There are people who spend years angry about a job loss, or in bitterness over something a family member did ages ago. These are people who go back into their past and pick up those hurts, and bring them into their current situation. And when you do this, you are setting up a stronghold for the lie of victimization, and giving the hurts of the past power over the truth of your current situation. These wounds are preventing you from moving into the plan God has for your life today, because you have given them the power to limit your ability to move forward. You are choosing to say, "I will continue to stay in that past place of hurt, hopelessness or despair, and let those feelings dominate my decisions today." Listen, there is a process of getting past a hurt, mourning, damage done, but if you are years down the road from whatever caused that wound, you need to reevaluate your processing. It is time to start looking through the windshield and get your eyes off the rearview mirror.

So let's talk about the lies that are hiding in your belief system if the stronghold of victimization is in place:

- Lie – Because I am a product of my past, I am still defined by my past.

    – It is true that things happened to us in our past, but we must use those things to move forward instead of being held back by them. I am not defined by the past rape, job loss, death in the family or divorce. Instead, I use those things to move forward.

- Lie – What happened to me before will mostly like happen again.

– The victim mentality says that things cannot change. This is a lie. I *can* take steps to prevent things that hurt me in the past from happening again, or prepare to deal with them differently.

- Lie – I am different from everyone else because my life is harder than everyone else's.

– You have no idea what others have been through. Many people have been through worse but have not told you their story yet. It doesn't matter how bad your experience was, there will most likely always be someone who has an equal or worse struggle.

- Lie – I deserve attention, notoriety and possibly even money because of my past struggles.

– Our society loves to sensationalize our past struggles. We sue other people because of what has happened to us. We go on TV shows, and tell our stories. We actually pay people money to tell their horror stories, and they become reality stars. Our society encourages this! Some of the stories are legitimate tragedies, but often times this preoccupation with the past just leads us to think we should get attention because of *our* story.

> - Lie – Once you hear my victim story, your expectation of me will be lowered, so I am not held accountable for an amazing future.

– Look at what Paul endured and yet he is still regarded today as a leader of our faith!

> - Lie – My identity comes from my experiences, not from how the Word of God identifies me.

– The Word of God may say that I am an overcomer, a victor, a warrior, a child of God, but if I think that because of my struggles I am none of these things, I am believing a lie.

> - Lie – Because I am a victim, I can reject my identity in Christ, and it is reasonable for me to gossip, hate, or be bitter. These sins are justifiable under the circumstances.

– This is a hard truth, but often times we think we can justify these sins because we have a story that allows us to be bitter or gossip about others. It is not okay to accept these sins because of past pain.

See if you agree with or relate to any of the following statements. If so, a stronghold of victimization may have a hiding place in your belief system.

1. I blame others
2. I regularly repeat the story of how I was hurt.

3. I feel like everything is working against me.
4. I do not believe I can fix the problems in my life.
5. I do not see that I have any responsibility for painful things that happened to me.
6. When I pray, I find I'm almost always complaining to God, and asking Him why He isn't fixing my problems.

When you're praying, always remember that there is a fine line between praying and complaining. Nowhere in the Bible does it say to "whine, in Jesus name." If your prayers consist of little but complaints and are always focused on you, it's a pretty sure sign you are believing some lies of the enemy and accepting the role of victim. And you know what? Being a victim is idolatry. Now, *that* is a sobering statement, but consider what it means to have a victim mentality. We worship the idol of self. Everything becomes about *me*, and how others need to consider *me*, and about drawing attention to *myself*. When *I* become the center of my world, I have made an idol out of me.

Here is probably the toughest thing to address on the subject of victim mentality. What is my real motivation for telling my story? There are really only two motivations for telling your victim story. One is, to encourage someone else who is going through a trial. In other words, I am telling you my story so you can see that others have been through similar trials and made it through happy, healthy and whole. I am telling you my story to encourage you. If that is not your motivation for telling your story, then it is the second reason; you want to manipulate someone. You are telling your story so that you can receive something from another person. You may be looking for pity, lowered expectations, money, attention, or perhaps time. In other words, you aren't telling your story to help someone else, you are telling your story to benefit yourself.

In John 5 there is a pool called Bethesda. As the story goes, when the water stirred, whoever was first into the water would be healed.

> *After these things there was a feast of the Jews, and Jesus went up to Jerusalem. Now there is in Jerusalem by the sheep gate a pool, which is called in Hebrew Bethesda, having five porticoes. In these lay a multitude of those who were sick, blind, lame, and withered, [waiting for the moving of the waters; for an angel of the Lord went down at certain seasons into the pool and stirred up the water; whoever then first, after the stirring up of the water, stepped in was made well from whatever disease with which he was afflicted.] A man was there who had been ill for thirty-eight years. When Jesus saw him lying there, and knew that he had already been a long time in that condition, He said to him, "Do you wish to get well?" The sick man answered Him, "Sir, I have no man to put me into the pool when the water is stirred up, but while I am coming, another steps down before me." Jesus said to him, "Get up, pick up your pallet and walk." Immediately the man became well, and picked up his pallet and began to walk.*
>
> (John 5:1-9)

This Scripture is a heart-wrenching story about a man who was lame. It is real and it is difficult not to have true compassion for this man. He states he has been this way thirty-eight years and says that no one will get him into the pool for his healing. This man may or may not have had a victim mentality; it is hard to tell from the story. But the process of healing from being a victim is clear, so we are looking at this story from the perspective of learning how to deal with the victim mentality. It starts with the question, "Do you wish to get well?" In other words, do you want to stay in the state you are in, or do you want to move into a different, future state? Do you want to move *out* of slavery or continue with slavery *in* you? This is a critical question for those with a victim mentality to answer. Do you wish to continue as you are, or are you willing to move out of that mentality?

Jesus then makes a simple and profound statement. He says, "Get up." He tells the man that he needs to get up. He does not need this pool. He does not need to continue to see things from the ground perspective. He needs to see things from a higher perspective. He is saying to the man, "You are looking at everything from the bottom looking up, and you need to be looking from the top down." He tells the man He wants him to have a new perspective.

Then He says to the man, "Pick up your pallet." Why does He say this? If the man is going to get healed he will no longer need the pallet, so why have him pick it up? Could it be that Jesus was saying that the man's identity was *in* the pallet; that the pallet defined the man as a cripple? The pallet showed the people around the man that he was a cripple and he was destined to stay on the ground. Jesus basically said, "It's time to give up your blankie!"

Consider this -- Jesus did not have to tell the man to pick it up at all. He could have just left it on the ground, as it was no longer needed. Jesus could have picked the pallet up himself. He could have said, "Hey I'll get this for you since you won't be needing it anymore." But instead, He looked at the man and said, "*You* pick it up. *You* need to be the one who relinquishes the thing that identifies you as a cripple. You need to relinquish that mentality."

Finally, Jesus says, "Walk." Now here's a fact – every time you walk, you end up in a different place from where you were. It's the weirdest thing about walking. You cannot walk and stay where you are! Jesus is saying, "You don't need to be here, lying by the pool, identified as a cripple. You need to get up, pick up your pallet and walk out of here. You need to be in a different place, not the place of a cripple, not the place of a helpless victim. You need to walk into your future!" Jesus is saying its time to put down that identity that you derived from your past hurt. Get up, and walk into a victor state of mind. You need to walk out of Egypt into a promised land!

Now, some will say, "But hey, you don't know how hard my past has been!" So lets go back into Scripture and see who had to deal with a hard past and what they did about it.

I see a man named Joseph who was hated by his brothers. His brothers hated him so much that they threw him into a well, sold him into slavery and lied to their dad about what happened to him. Now *that* is family trauma! Then, as he is rising to authority in Egypt, he is falsely accused by Pharaoh's wife and thrown into jail. In jail, although he interprets other prisoners' dreams, and asks to be remembered when they are released, he is actually forgotten and left there for two more years. Joseph, however, ends up being second in command in all of Egypt and saves his family, as well as the people of Egypt, from starvation!

I see a guy named Joshua. He comes out of slavery and

112

travels across a desert with a bunch of discontented people. He is selected to scout out the Promised Land, and he delivers the message, "YES! We can take the land!" But because of the people around him who will not trust God, the decision is made to not go forward, and Joshua is stranded in the desert for forty more years. But this man ends up being the commander of all of Israel, and leads them into a conquest of the land God promised His people!

I see a woman named Ruth. Her husband dies, her father-in-law dies, and her brother-in-law dies. She has to leave her people and her native country to live in a foreign land where she will not be respected. She has to work gleaning wheat from a field, dependent on her mother-in-law. She has to humble herself and take a chance by presenting herself at the feet of Boaz. She ends up, however, married to a very wealthy and respectable man and is in the lineage of Jesus Christ, Savior of all man!

I see a man named Paul; a well-educated man who gets dropped to the ground and told he will have to serve the very person he has been persecuting. He's arrested, put on trial, stoned, driven out of numerous towns, shipwrecked, even bitten by a snake, and he ends up writing down the majority of the New Covenant, so you and I can learn about our Savior today!

I know another guy. He came from divorced parents; his father never told him that he loved him. On two occasions, when he argued with his older brother, his father made them fist fight in public to settle the argument! No disrespect to the father, but these are the facts. His dad died at the age of forty-eight, when the man was only twenty-six years old. The guy's mother died of brain cancer. His father, mother-in-law, grandmother and grand father-in-law all died within an eighteen month period. His wife, of a twenty-year relationship, died from cancer in his arms, leaving him a single father with two little girls. He had been laid off from good jobs and fired from six figure jobs. As a pastor, this man was forced to resign from a church that he co-founded. Now, why do I tell you that particular story? Because I really don't care about all that! It is in my past! Today, I have the honor of being the pastor of one of the most exciting and dynamic churches in South Florida! I am remarried to a wonderful, God loving, co-laboring, beautiful woman! My daughters are two strong, Christian, Jesus loving, amazing women! God loves me! I am eternally saved! God has great plans and a great destiny for me! Why in the world would I want to look in the review mirror? And regardless of what *your* story is, why would *you*? I am not being insensitive here. I have been there, I have been hurt, I have had struggles, but if I let them define who I am then I will not walk into who I can be!

But let me tell you about one last guy in the Bible. At birth, He has to run for His life. He is rejected by the people in His own hometown, and He is arrested by the people He came to serve. He is tried unfairly, He is beaten, and His beard is pulled out. He gets spit on, mocked, has a crown of thorns placed on His head, and is forced to carry His own cross to the place where they crucify Him, among thieves, despite the fact that He is innocent. A great victim story isn't it? But this Man doesn't get bogged down by His past, or spend any time looking back. He doesn't identify Himself as a victim. This guy keeps His eyes focused solely on the plan God has for Him – being THE KING OF KINGS AND THE LORD OF LORDS!

If you cannot get yourself past your past, then you cannot get excited about the future that God is excited about *for you*! There is so much more ahead of you than what lies behind!

So, get up! Pick up your pallet! And walk!

Eight

Stronghold of Unworthiness

We've been talking about lies that the enemy places in our belief system, and how we have to expose those places of hiding so the lie is revealed, thereby making that hiding place useless for the enemy in the future. So I want to paint this scenario and see if this is true for any of you. Sometimes our prayers are not getting answered or we don't see the answers. We are laying things up before God, and we are trying to ask God for things that we believe are righteous, but we don't seem to be getting answers so we start to get concerned. One of the very first thoughts we have is, "Did I do something wrong?" Then the thought progresses to, "I wonder if there is something I've done wrong, so God is withholding the answer from me until I get this thing cleaned up." And then to, "Right now, I feel unworthy because I've messed up, and I think I'm in a phase of punishment with God, and He is not going to give me the answer until I clean up my life."

Have you ever gotten into that scenario we Christians call the dry spell, where you're just not feeling close to God? You've lobbed some things out there and you're saying to God, "Could you show me, could you give me direction, could you answer these questions that I have?" But those answer don't come. So you begin to struggle; why am I not getting direction on these things I'm asking God about, when they are things I'd expect Him to want me to know or do?

When *I'm* struggling, here's where I often times go – I have to figure out what it is I've done wrong that has stopped the communication between God and me, because I think He can't or won't talk to me until I put this thing on the table, and confess and repent of it. So then I go through this time of searching my memory; is there something I did? Is there an attitude of some sort, am I not studying enough, my quiet time not real? What is going on that God would keep the answers from coming? I turn the whole thing back on myself and think, as soon as I figure out what's wrong with me, *then* God will be able to talk. Does anybody else deal with that? Does anybody else turn it back on himself and say, "I must be doing something wrong because God's not talking to me, and I don't know what to do"?

The stronghold we're dealing with in this game of Hide and Seek is the stronghold of unworthiness; feeling unworthy of God speaking to you, feeling unworthy of God loving you. Not feeling worthy of God's giving you direction. Here's a question I have for you – when you came to the conclusion that you are unworthy, who made that decision? Who is judging your worthiness or unworthiness? Who makes the assessment that what you did in the past or what you are currently doing is keeping God from talking to you? Who determines your worthiness to approach God?

The next Sabbath nearly the whole city assembled to hear the word of the Lord. But when the Jews saw the crowds, they were filled with jealousy and began contradicting the things spoken by Paul, and were blaspheming. Paul and Barnabas spoke out boldly and said, "It is necessary that the word of God be spoken

117

to you first; since you repudiate it and judge yourselves unworthy of eternal life, behold, we are turning to the Gentiles."

(Acts 13:44-46.)

That's a very bold statement Paul makes. What he is saying is, "I've been sharing the gospel with you for quite a while. I've been talking about His love, His grace, His goodness, His joy, His sacrifice, His forgiveness, and His reconciliation. I've been talking to you about eternal life, and you decided you weren't worthy of that eternal life." See, I think too often *we* decide we are unworthy before God. *We* determine that we are unworthy and, guess what, it's not up to us. *It's not up to you!* So here's my question – are you worthy on your own to stand before God? The answer is no. And that is actually a great thing! It is great because it's actually part of the beautiful redemption story – the story that tells us that we alone, in and of ourselves, are *not* worthy to stand before God. You'll see why that's a beautiful thing in a bit.

When He had completed all His discourse in the hearing of the people, He went to Capernaum. And a centurion's slave, who was highly regarded by him, was sick and about to die. When he heard about Jesus, he sent some Jewish elders asking Him to come and save the life of his slave. When they came to Jesus, they earnestly implored Him, saying, "He is worthy for You to grant this to him; for he loves our nation and it was he who built us our synagogue." Now Jesus started on His way with them; and when He was not far from the house, the centurion sent friends, saying to Him, "Lord, do not trouble Yourself further, for I am not worthy for You to come under my roof; for this reason

I did not even consider myself worthy to come to You, but just say the word, and my servant will be healed. For I also am a man placed under authority, with soldiers under me; and I say to this one, 'Go!' and he goes, and to another, 'Come!' and he comes, and to my slave, 'Do this!' and he does it." Now when Jesus heard this, He marveled at him, and turned and said to the crowd that was following Him, "I say to you, not even in Israel have I found such great faith."

(Luke 7:1-9.)

Other people saw the centurion as worthy because of the things he had done. He had built the synagogue so he was worthy to have God answer his prayers. But the centurion himself said, "I am not worthy," because he recognized that this was not about him and what he could do; it was about Jesus and what *He* could do. He was saying, "*I know what Jesus can do.*" In other words, the centurion had more confidence in getting an answer through the worthiness of Jesus than his own worthiness. The centurion was saying, "My worthiness is not enough but Jesus' worthiness is." And the servant got healed.

Basically, this man who has never been offered salvation – he's a gentile; Jesus hasn't even come to him yet so he's not a child of God who could have all these reasons as to why he is unworthy – is now saying of Jesus, "I am not, but He *is* worthy, so I will go to Him." Did Jesus heal the servant because the centurion was worthy? No. Even though Jesus said, "I've never seen faith like this..," He never called him worthy. He healed the servant because the centurion had faith. He did it because the centurion said, "It's not about my worthiness it's about Yours." The answer came through Jesus' alone; it had nothing to do with the centurion's worthiness or unworthiness, only that he believed.

And Jesus said to the centurion, "Go; it shall be done for you as you have believed." And the servant was healed that very moment."

(Matthew 8:13.)

The centurion got his answer even though he felt unworthy, because he believed in Jesus' worthiness. So you and I can feel unworthy, yet believe in what Jesus can do because of *His* worthiness.

Then I looked, and I heard the voice of many angels around the throne and the living creatures and the elders; and the number of them was myriads of myriads, and thousands of thousands, saying with a loud voice, "Worthy is the Lamb that was slain to receive power and riches and wisdom and might and honor and glory and blessing."

(Revelation 5:11-12.)

Look at this – "*Worthy is the Lamb that was slain.*" That's a chronological statement. *Was* slain, as in past tense. So we are in a time, chronologically, during which the Lamb *has* worthiness, because the Lamb was slain. The Lamb was Jesus, and that means you and I now know somebody who is worthy. *Worthy is the Lamb,* and it's all about the Lamb, and when you get your thoughts on the worthy Lamb, you will see what the worthy Lamb can do for you. What does He deserve to receive because He is worthy? Scripture says He deserves to receive power, riches, wisdom, might, honor, glory and blessing.

I'm going to break down each of these words for you in Greek:

– Power: Dunamis: Strength and ability.
– Riches: Poutos: Abundance of possessions.
– Wisdom: Sophia: Full of supreme intelligence.
– Might: Ischus: Force
– Honor: Time: A reverence due to rank.
– Glory: Doxa: The most exalted state, splendor, brightness and majesty.
– Blessing: Eulogia: Praise or laudation; worthy of praise.

So Revelation 5:12 says that Jesus the Lamb has received, because He was slain, strength, and an abundance of possessions. He is full of supreme intelligence, He is forceful, there is a reverence due Him because He is the most exalted state of splendor and majesty, and He is due praise. So all we're talking about right now is the worthiness of the Lamb. It is Jesus who is this worthy. It is Jesus who has received all these things. And once you understand the significance of Jesus being worthy, you can get off the thoughts of yourself and get them on the Lamb.

Consider this; what could you have done before God to be worthy anyway? What could you possibly have done to be worthy before God? Here's what I mean by that – when I go back into the Old Testament and I look at those who tried to become worthy under the law, I see that no one succeeded. No one became worthy before God under the law. As a matter of fact, that is why Jesus came to fulfill the law. He was the only One who could have accomplished that; He was the only one worthy under the law. When you look at believers over the thousands of years since then, we never hear of one example of someone who was worthy before God. Let me ask you this question; how many of us have sinned and fallen short of the glory of God? ALL of us. So what that means is that there is not a single one of us who will ever be worthy on our own before God. So why are we talking to ourselves? What would be the point of convincing myself that I am not worthy? Maybe I'd be better off asking myself, "Did you have to prove yourself worthy to be saved?"

Now think about this:

But God demonstrates His own love toward us, in that while we were yet sinners, Christ died for us.

(Romans 5:8.)

At that point in your life, before salvation, you were rebellious against God. You were defiant toward God, you were disrespectful of the things of God, and you didn't want anything to do with Him. You certainly didn't want to do anything God was asking you to do; yet though you were in that state, Jesus died for you anyway. Now if that is true – and I believe that it is true that you don't have to prove yourself worthy to be saved – then why would you have to prove yourself worthy in order for Him to continue to love you? As a father, which would be easier for you to love: a rebellious, sinful son or a son who is a follower of God? But which would be easier for God to love: a rebellious, sinful child or a child that's trying to follow Him? The answer is neither is easier to love; He loves them both. He doesn't have more love for this one than that one; He loves us all. He invites us all equally! Even while you were defiant towards God, He loved you and was reaching out to you. And if that were the case then, why would you think He would stop now? God loved and accepted you while you were rebelling against Him, so He will surely love and accept you while you are trying to follow Him.

But I still feel unworthy. Sometimes I still turn this thing around on myself and think, "I must have done something wrong because this isn't working. I just feel unworthy; there is something in me that's not measuring up."

I have been crucified with Christ; and it is no longer I who live, but Christ lives in me; and the life which I now live in the flesh I live by faith in the Son of God, who loved me and gave Himself up for me.

(Galatians 2:20.)

What that scripture just said was that you can convince yourself you are unworthy, but the worthy One lives in you. The one who *is* worthy to stand before God lives in you, so worthiness lives in you. The worthiness in you is Christ, and if Christ makes you worthy then stop convincing yourself otherwise. What happens is we say, "Oh, I've gotten in the way of things because I've messed things up." But think about how arrogant that statement is. Here's what it says – *I* have the ability to mess up, and that ability outweighs the ability of the One who has all strength, the abundance of possession, who is full of supreme intelligence, who is forceful and who has reverence due Him; *I* can mess up in a way that overshadows *Him*. That is so broken. It is so broken to think that your shortcoming is greater than His glory – that your mess-up is greater than His worthiness. That your fallibility is greater than His majesty. He is living in you, and if you think that you are greater than Jesus you have a terribly wrong, inflated opinion of yourself. If Christ lives in you and you are going to deem yourself unworthy because of your mistake, then you are saying Christ's worthiness is not greater than any mistake you could make.

*The angel of the Lord appeared to him and said to him,
"The Lord is with you, O valiant warrior."*

(Judges 6:12.)

Let me say this, the Old Testament is always – every single
story – *always* a physical representation that helps us grasp a
spiritual concept of the new covenant. In the previous verse it
says, "The Lord is with you..." If you're a believer today, is
the Lord with you? Yes! He will never leave you or forsake
you. So here the Lord says to Gideon, "I am with you, O
valiant warrior."

*Then Gideon said to Him, "O my lord, if the Lord is
with us, why then has all this happened to us? And
where are all His miracles which our fathers told us
about, saying, 'Did not the Lord bring us up from
Egypt?' But now the Lord has abandoned us and given
us into the hand of Midian." The Lord looked at him
and said, "Go in this your strength and deliver Israel
from the hand of Midian. Have I not sent you?"*

(Judges 6:13-14.)

The Scripture says, "The Lord looked at him." Now let me
ask if any of you had a father who gave you THAT look? The
look that said, "Don't make me come over there." You knew if
you got that look, you better pay attention. I imagine, however,
with Jesus being the loving Jesus that He is, this was most
likely a much more intense moment than even that. He was
probably saying, "Come here, Gideon. I'm going to speak into
you, and I want you to hear what I'm about to say." So He
looks at him, and then He goes on to say, "Go in this your
strength." What does He mean when He says, "This your

strength?" Was He saying to Gideon, "You're a big enough guy, you'll be fine, just get some food, run down to that camp and whack a few of them with your sword?" No. If you punctuate it the way Jesus would have spoken it, it would read, "Go in THIS YOUR STRENGTH." He was saying *THIS* is your strength – *the fact that I am with you.* In other words, "The Lord is with you, Gideon, therefore go with *Me* as your strength."

Now, while Gideon is standing there doubting himself and thinking he is unqualified and unworthy to be a leader, the Lord continues and says to him, "Have I not sent you?" And then He says, "Surely I'll be with you." Did He not just tell him again? Did He not just say again, "Listen, Gideon, this is not about you. *I, the Lord,* am sending you, and that is the reason you'll be able to do this. Surely I'll be with you, and you will defeat Midian."

I don't know if you noticed, but the angel of the Lord never answered his questions or refuted his whining. He never stopped and said, "You know, Gideon, let me tell you about where the Lord is; that His timing is different from your timing, and that's why you think He's not there." In addition, He never said, "Yeah, I know you Midianite guys are weaker ... and you're smaller ... and you're kinda puny." Listen, He has no desire to address our whining, because our whining is evidence that we have a lack of faith in Him.

If you and I know that Christ is in us, then isn't any determination that we make about our own unworthiness at war with that? I'll even go so far as to say that you are *demeaning the value of Christ in you* by judging yourself unworthy. You *are* worthy. You are worthy because He is with you and *that's* the strength in which you go. Because He is worthy I don't have to assess my unworthiness, I just have to walk in His. See, here's the struggle we have. We believe that if we walk righteously, then Christ will live in us. If I believe that Christ will live in me *because* I'm walking righteously, then I have it backwards. The reality is that because Christ lives in me, I *can* walk righteously. I can't do it on my own; I'm unworthy on my own. But He is worthy to be righteous because He who knew no sin became sin so that I might become righteous with God in Him.

So what's the lie hiding in my belief system? It is that my right standing with God comes from how righteously I act, when the truth is, that my right standing with God comes from the righteousness of Jesus. Because Jesus is righteous, I am right before God. Now, instead of trying to be good, I learn how to be the valiant warrior that I am in Christ. He has already called me to be a valiant warrior; that's the beauty of the story of Gideon. Gideon shows us that if we assess it on our own we will consider ourselves unworthy, and that doesn't matter to God. What God says is, "I know who you are. I know who you are, *valiant warrior*. Though you have no idea, I know what you are about to do. You're assessing your ability to accomplish whatever this is, and I'm telling you that you've already done it. You've already done it and I'm going to walk you through it."

> *Therefore let us draw near with confidence to the throne of grace, so that we may receive mercy and find grace to help in time of need.*
>
> (Hebrews 4:16.)

Don't miss the last words of this verse, because most

people are looking for mercy and grace. Look why you're getting the mercy and grace – "To help me in my time of need." You remember that desert place where we started? You know what God is saying in these moments? He's saying that we have no confidence when we're going to him. You know when your kids come to you and say, "Well, you know Dad (or Mom), I've messed up, and I'm not really a good kid, and I know I don't have a lot of value to you, but could you help me with this?" In moments like that I think, man, that's not the kid *I* raised. I want to tell them that they're stronger than that, that I see more in them than that. What I want them to do is come to me and say, "Dad, I know you are here to help, and this is what I need." Of course! Absolutely. I'm all in; I want to help!

If we are not approaching God with confidence, then we are bringing our unworthiness. And here's what we're saying to Him – "God, I want to come and talk to you but I'm going to leave Jesus over there somewhere. I just want to come before you on my own merits, and this is what I see, God; that I'm unworthy and that I just can't do it." And God is saying, "Where's Jesus in all of that?! Jesus is the One that makes you worthy; He's the One that makes you righteous. Have confidence in that, and you'll get the help you need."

When God created this earth years and years and years ago, He created it with love. He put plants on it, He put water on it, He put animals on it, and then He made man. When He did all of these things He did it out of love. He just wanted to pour His love out on mankind. He said this planet is yours. You have dominion over it, eat what you want (except for one tree), go and name the animals, have dominion over every living creature; this is your domain. God gave man a garden and said, "I want to spend time with you, Adam. I'll walk with you in

Eden." But God also told Adam to not eat from the tree, because if he did eat from the tree it would be in direct disobedience to God – and that disobedience would show God that Adam had chosen to heeds Satan's words rather than His own. This would fracture the relationship between God and man by establishing a relationship between Satan and man.

Some people will ask why He put the tree there in the first place? Why did He give us the opportunity to become separated from Him? Because God understands love. He knows that if you don't have an option then you can't truly love. If you don't have an option then you can't say, yes God, I want *you*. I *choose you*. How many people would actually want to be married to their spouse if they had no choice *other* than to be married to them? You would rather know that they *chose* you, wouldn't you? That they made the choice to love you. So this is what God was saying, "I love you, and if you want to show Me your love every day, just stay away from that tree." Then Satan came in, the great deceiver. He went to Eve and asked if she wanted to be more like God. Satan told Eve that she would be more like God if she ate from that tree, because then she would know good from evil. Satan is a cunning and convincing liar, so Eve thought, "Of course! Yeah! That tree would make us wise, so maybe it *is* the right thing to do!

So what happened? Eve stopped listening to God, and started following Satan's direction. Satan had twisted God's word and planted a lie in Eve's belief system, and when Adam and Eve decided to eat from that tree they chose to follow Satan rather than God. That broke their loving relationship with God. It broke His heart. But God, not wanting them to be separated from Him for eternity by their sin, stepped in and said He could fix the separated relationship. This is why He sent Jesus, so that Jesus could pay the consequences and take the punishment for sin for you and for me. Jesus took our condemnation on the cross so that we could be in right standing with God again. He, who knew no sin, became sin so that we might become the righteousness of God in Him.

Jesus came; He was scorned, beaten, and whipped at a post. He had a crown of thorns put on His head, His beard was ripped out; He was publicly humiliated as He was nailed up on the cross. Then He was crucified, and died. Why is that important? Because God had a cup of wrath, that was the punishment for all sin, and He poured that cup out on Jesus. As Jesus was dying, He said, "My God, my God, why have you forsaken me?" because at that moment, He was *becoming* sin for man, and that separated Him from God. The beauty of this story is that He doesn't stay dead. He goes to hell, but then comes back having conquered death and hell, and the separation from God. In having done this He is declaring, "I have overcome this for you so I can now give you eternal life." He was forgiven in His death and justified in His resurrection. This means that because Christ is risen, I put my faith in the fact that He died for me to pay for my sins. He was raised again so that I appear spotless, as though I have never sinned, so that I can now be justified in Christ and have eternal life.

Remember when we said earlier that *not* being worthy in and of yourself was a beautiful thing because it is part of the redemption story? Now you see you don't have to be worthy because Jesus took your condemnation and gave you *His* status, and *that is* a beautiful thing!

So what is the offer today? The offer today is that if you don't recognize Christ in you then you need to be restored with

God. The only way you can be restored with God is through Jesus, because He is the only worthy one. He is the only one that never sinned, the only one that never broke His relationship with God while He was here on earth. Now He can stand in a righteous position and say, "I will take the condemned status of (*insert your name here,*) and I will give him or her my status of righteousness." Jesus says that He will take all of our punishment on Himself, so that when we stand before God and God asks if we want an eternity with Him, we can say, "Yes! Jesus took the punishment I deserved. There is no separation due me. I am coming in His name. I am covered in Jesus." And God will say, "Well done. You are made worthy through Him."

Listen, you are *not* worthy because of you. Stop focusing on yourself and trying to figure out what you are doing wrong. You are worthy because of Christ *in you*; so don't convince yourself otherwise or you will demean the value of Christ's sacrifice, and His presence in you!

Because of the righteousness of God in you, you have the opportunity to be a valiant warrior.

So what are you waiting for? Go be one!

Nine

Stronghold of Pride

If we were to look up the word "pride" in English, Hebrew and Greek, we would find the following words and definitions:

> ENGLISH: (pride) a feeling of deep pleasure or satisfaction derived from one's own achievements
> HEBREW: (Ga own) arrogance
> GREEK: (huperafanea) self exaltation (self absorption)

Arrogance is the puffing up of a soul, or loftiness. In other words, it is an empty assurance which trusts in its own power and resources, and shamefully despises and violates divine laws.

In the United States, we like the term self-confidence, which is a feeling of trust in one's own abilities, qualities and judgement. Another term we like is self-esteem; a favorable opinion of one's own worth or abilities. These are good things right? We want our kids to grow up with self-confidence and a healthy self-esteem. We want them to be self motivated and accomplish great things. We want them to have a sense that they're not limited; they can do anything they set their minds to. And we do not want them to shrink back, be shy, or intimidated by life. So what's the difference between these healthy, positive attitudes and pride?

I believe pride was the very first sin ever committed, and when you look at the following Scriptures about satan you'll see why. Remember as you read these, that pride is trusting in your own power.

How you have fallen from heaven (satan – see Revelation 20) *O star of the morning, son of the dawn! You have been cut down to the earth, You who have weakened the nations! But you said in your heart, "I will ascend to heaven; I will raise my throne above the stars of God, And I will sit on the mount of assembly in the recesses of the north. I will ascend above the heights of the clouds; I will make myself like the Most High." Nevertheless you will be thrust down to Sheol, to the recesses of the pit.*

(Isaiah 14:12-15.)

You were the anointed cherub who covers, And I placed you there. You were on the holy mountain of God; You walked in the midst of the stones of fire. You were blameless in your ways From the day you were created Until unrighteousness was found in you. By the abundance of your trade – (how well you were doing) *You were internally filled with violence, And you sinned; Therefore I have cast you as profane From the mountain of God. And I have destroyed you, O covering cherub, From the midst of the stones of fire. Your heart was lifted up because of your beauty; You corrupted your wisdom by reason of your splendor.*

(Ezekiel 28:14-17.)

This verse says that satan was filled with violence. That word in Hebrew is *chamac*, and one definition of chamac is "injustice." In other words, satan wanted equality with the Most High which would have been an injustice. It goes on to say, *"Your heart was lifted up because of your beauty,"* or translated, "You began to think highly of yourself." These are the verses that show us what I believe is the first sin – pride. You see, Adam and Eve were the first humans to sin, but satan's pride caused God to cast him out of heaven and down to earth before Adam and Eve were in the garden. Therefore, it is satan who actually committed the first sin.

But let's consider what was at the core of his sin. Satan believed he could become like God. Notice the Scripture does not say he wants God's position; he just wants to be like him. Now with that said, do you think God was intimidated by the threat of satan being like Him? Do you think God would kick him out of heaven because He was worried satan might take over His throne? That's almost a silly thought. God was the creator of all things. He was almighty, powerful and majestic. In no way did God fear satan or consider him competition. The issue was the sin of pride. Satan believed that by his own efforts and on his own merit he could rise to such a lofty place.

Consider the five "I will" statements of satan. "I will ascend … I will raise my throne … I will sit on the mount … I will ascend above … I will make myself like the Most Hight." Do you see it? Do you see the pride in these statements? Satan is not suggesting that God could elevate him, he is suggesting that he can do this on his own. Remember the English translation of the word pride: … *satisfaction derived from one's* own *achievements*. So pride is depending on *yourself* for spiritual elevation! And for this sin, God rejects satan and casts him out of heaven.

Because satan's belief system includes this pride (this self elevation pride,) and achieving equality with God is still his highest priority, it is obvious what some of his follow-on actions will be. He will continue to try to accomplish these things on his own efforts, but if he cannot succeed he will try to make sure you are rejected by God also. He will want to draw you away from the God who rejected him. You can see his strategy play out in the garden of Eden with Adam and Eve. Notice his first conversation with Eve about the tree.

> The serpent said to the woman, "You surely will not die! For God knows that in the day you eat from it your eyes will be opened, and you will be like God, knowing good and evil."
>
> (Genesis 3:4-5.)

Do you see his tactics? What is he saying to Eve? "You can be like God!" Is that not exactly what HE wanted? And by the way, when satan says to Eve, "the day you eat from it your eyes will be opened....," he is telling Eve that it is up to her, and that she can accomplish becoming like God based on her own efforts. He is trying to convince Eve that she should commit the same sin he did, thereby making sure she is also rejected by God.

But God warns against this; He says that because He is opposed to us trying to accomplish things on our own merits, we are to resist the devil and receive His grace. See it in this Scripture:

135

But He gives a greater grace. Therefore it says, "God is opposed to the proud, but gives grace to the humble." Submit therefore to God. Resist the devil and he will flee from you. Draw near to God and He will draw near to you.

(James 4:6-8.)

Do you see that God gives grace, but is opposed to the proud? I do not believe that humility is the opposite of pride. Anyone can have humility. There are plenty of humble people out there. But look at the definition of humble: not rising from the ground. Consider this, if pride is what you can accomplish on your own, then the opposite is grace. The fact that you cannot accomplish it on your own is why you need grace. Grace is getting what you do not deserve and what you did not accomplish on your own.

Pride says, "*I do not need* God because *I can do* what He does." Pride says, "*I am fully capable* of accomplishing what I want to do *under my own* power." Pride is all about leaning on oneself, with an exaggerated opinion of one's own merit.

Grace on the other hand, is the *unmerited* favor of God. It says you can accomplish nothing by your own merit, *nothing on your own*. And the fact that you cannot accomplish it on your own makes it clear you need grace, because grace is receiving from God what you do not deserve, and accomplishing what you could not do through your own strength and capabilities.

Unfortunately, the proud do not get grace. They do not understand it. They have no need for it. They are self reliant and believe they can accomplish *anything they desire* without God. This is why God is profoundly against pride – because it rejects His grace! He is offering something amazing to the proud and they are saying no thank you, I can get what I need or want on my own without you, God. God says pride takes away His ability to show you grace. God is saying if this is about what *you* can do, then it is not about what I can do *for* you. This is the entire message of Jesus Christ! What we could not do for ourselves, God did for us in Jesus Christ. We can not earn it, accomplish it, or do it on our own.

So do you see that you cannot receive grace without humility, but humility is not the antidote for pride? We need to be humble and submit to God in order to be open to His grace, and we need to resist pride in order for God to draw near to us and give us His unmerited favor. But humility alone is no substitution for grace.

So, what made God so angry that He cast satan out of heaven? Satan's pride in himself, thus his rejection of God's grace. And what will cause many of *us* to be cast out of heaven for eternity? The same thing – rejecting God's grace – because pride causes us to reject what God is freely offering us. So how does man receive an eternity with God in heaven? Simply by accepting God's grace.

Most of us think about pride in a demonstrative way. We think of someone spewing out boastful comments, sticking out his chest, or demanding recognition, but the reality is that pride is also much less than that. In truth, pride is simply a feeling that we can or have accomplished something based on our own efforts, whether we outwardly demonstrate that belief or not. We make statements like, *"I WILL not be like my mother or father." "I Will financially succeed." "I WILL never do that stupid thing again."* These are all prideful statements. They are perhaps admirable sentiments, but all are solely focused and reliant on your own abilities. Pride is self-centeredness in all its forms.

With that being said, is the right thing to do to always end a statement like that with, "If God wills"? Most of the time the answer is no. You see, we should know the will of God; He left it for us in writing. He left it in two testaments. His will and testaments are there so we can know the will of God. And since we know His will, we don't have to question if something *is* His will. Maybe the right thing to do is to walk in the belief that God is in a place higher than I am, and I cannot accomplish a spiritual elevation without Him. I am incapable of accomplishing what God can easily accomplish. This is God's truth, and it says, "It is a lie to think I do not need God in everything I do."

King David understood this:

Bless the Lord, O my soul, And all that is within me, bless His holy name. Bless the Lord, O my soul, And forget none of His benefits; Who pardons all your iniquities, Who heals all your diseases; Who redeems your life from the pit, Who crowns you with lovingkindness and compassion; Who satisfies your years with good things, So that your youth is renewed like the eagle. The Lord performs righteous deeds And judgments for all who are oppressed. He made known His ways to Moses, His acts to the sons of Israel. The Lord is compassionate and gracious, Slow to anger and abounding in lovingkindness. He will not always strive with us, nor will He keep His anger forever. He has not dealt with us according to our sins, Nor rewarded us according to our iniquities. For as high as the heavens are above the earth, So great is His lovingkindness toward those who fear Him.

(Psalm 103, Underlined emphasis mine.)

Over and over in this scripture David reminds us of what God does: He gives benefits, pardons inquities, heals diseases, redeems our life, crowns us, satisfies us with good, does righteous deeds, provides judgement for the oppressed. He's compassionate, gracious, slow to anger, and abounds in lovingkindness. David throws a massive blanket over what God does for us. He reminds us of all that God is doing, and all the things we need Him for, so we don't get into a place of thinking we can accomplish life on our own. Notice especially, the last verse. David says the Lord is high as the heavens and full of grace! That was the position satan originally enjoyed, but he chose to reject it.

Lies become strongholds in our belief system. They hide there and affect how we act. So what are the lies that build the stronghold of pride which affects our relationship with God? Pride is built on a lie that makes you believe you can achieve salvation through your own deeds. It is built on the lie that you are righteous based on your own actions, your own merits. It makes you believe that God's grace is due to your worthiness. The lie of pride says God needs *you – ouch!*

Pride brings temporary exaltation but an eternal downfall.

Satan even tried to tempt Jesus into being prideful. You will remember from Scripture that Jesus was tempted by the same things we are.

For we do not have a high priest who cannot sympathize with our weaknesses, but One who has been tempted in all things as we are, yet without sin.

(Hebrews 4:15.)

So what are the "all things" by which Jesus was tempted?

For all that is in the world, the lust of the flesh and the lust of the eyes and the boastful pride of life, is not from the Father, but is from the world.

(1 John 2:16.)

We are reminded of three things by which we in the world were tempted, and by which Jesus was also tempted: lust of the flesh, lust of the eyes, and pride of life. Let's look at an example:

Then Jesus was let up by the Spirit into the wilderness to be tempted by the devil. And after He had fasted forty days and forty nights, He then became hungry. And the tempter came and said to Him, "If You are the Son of God, command that these stones become bread." But He answered and said, "It is written, 'Man shall not live on bread alone, but on every word that proceeds out of the mouth of God.'" Then the devil took Him into the holy city and had Him stand on the pinnacle of the temple, and said to Him, "If You are the Son of God, throw Yourself down; for it is written, 'He will command His angels concerning You'; and 'On their hands they will bear You up, So that You will not strike Your foot against a stone.'" Jesus said to him, "On the other hand, it is written, 'You shall not put the Lord your God to the test.'" Again, the devil took Him to a very high mountain and showed Him all

140

the kingdoms of the world and their glory and he said to Him, "All these things I will give You, if You fall down and worship me." Then Jesus said to him, "Go, Satan! For it is written, 'You shall worship the Lord your God, and serve Him only.'"

(Matthew 4:1-10.)

Did you see the three? Lust of the flesh: make stone into bread. Lust of the eyes: see the kingdoms that can be yours. Pride of life: show everyone that you can jump and not be hurt. But even Jesus recognized His need for God. In His responses to satan, Jesus says, "We live on every word that proceeds out of the mouth of God. Do not test God," and "Worship only God." It is exactly that recognition of our need for God that extends God's grace to us.

The Bible is full of people who exemplify the ways in which God's grace is greater than pride.

- David – a shepherd not even considered for Samuel's call, but God made him King.
- Moses – a murderer whom God called to lead the people.
- Jacob - who held on, waiting for a blessing.
- The woman with the issue of blood – who needed a touch to be healed.
- Blind man – who cried out "Son of David have mercy on me."
- Sirophonecian woman – who said, "... even the dogs get crumbs from the masters table."
- Day of Pentecost – the people, who were pierced to the heart wanting salvation.
- Mary – who said, "May it be done to me according to your word."

- Namaan – who dipped seven times and was healed.
- Hannah – who cried out for a child.
- Peter (3 time failure) says – "To whom shall we go, you have the words of life?"
- Jarius – who falls at Jesus' feet for the sake of his servant.
- Zacheaus – who climbs a tree to see a Savior.
- John – who, in Revelations, falls as if dead before Jesus.
- Elders – who bow down before the throne.
- Joshua – who falls on his face before the angel of the Lord, before the Jericho battle.
- Elijah and Ezekiel – who fall on their faces before the Lord.

All of these people understood they could not accomplish what they needed on their own. All of these people understood that only God could accomplish what they needed. All were willing to stop their own efforts, and go to God.

Satan's strategy is to draw you away from God by making you believe you don't need Him and that you can do all things on your own. But pride will keep you from receiving God's grace. When we try to accomplish things on our own, we are formally announcing to God that we don't need His grace.

Rejection of God's grace is the only thing that can cause us to suffer eternally. The stronghold of pride stands in the way of accepting the grace that God provides, and it is through His grace *alone* that we can have eternal salvation.

Ten

Stronghold of Religion

Our enemy, according to Scripture, is cunning, wise and deceitful. So when he comes after us, it may not be as obvious as we would like it to be. Deceit means we are blinded to what is happening. Here's an interesting thought – satan has more experience dealing with human ways than humans have in dealing with satan's ways. In other words, he has been deceiving man for thousands of years, but we each have only about 10 to 70 years of experience dealing with *his* ways. He has been around for a long time watching how man thinks, how man makes his decisions, and what is effective in tempting man. He uses those thousands of years of knowledge as weaponry to come against us.

The stronghold of religion is probably the scariest stronghold of them all. The reason I say this is, the stronghold of religion is shrouded in even greater deception than most of the others and is much more compelling, because it plays at the very core of who we desire to be before our God. We desire to please God, to walk uprightly before Him, to serve God, and to walk in the authority of Jesus Christ, and satan knows this. So satan will come between us and God, using the very desire we have to be close to Him, to deceive us. By twisting the Word of God and twisting the truth of God, he is able to get us to believe something about God that is not true. Satan learns what you know.

> *Now the serpent was more crafty than any beast of the field which the Lord God had made. And he said to the woman, "Indeed, has God said, 'You shall not eat from any tree of the garden?'"*
>
> (Genesis 3:1.)

Think about that question. Satan is probing to find out what Eve knows and what she believes. He wants to know if God has told her that she should not eat from a particular tree. Notice, he did not ask "Do you know about the two special trees in the garden?" He asked if God had instructed her to not eat from *any* of the trees in the garden. In other words, "Do you have any requirements on you to not eat from any of the trees in the garden?" He is probing to find out what she has been told. He is not showing his hand that he knows she isn't supposed to eat from a certain tree. He is sizing up his adversary to see what his deception plan will be.

> *The woman said to the serpent, "From the fruit of the trees of the garden we may eat;* but *from the fruit of the tree which is in the middle of the garden, God has said, 'You shall not eat from it or touch it, or you will die.'"*
>
> (Genesis 3:2-3.)

Now satan has the information he needs to begin his attempt to deceive her. He knows what she knows so he can strategize accordingly. And watch how deceptive his approach is when it comes to Eve's relationship with God.

> *The serpent said to the woman, "You surely will not die! For God knows that in the day you eat from it your eyes will be opened, and you will be like God,*

145

knowing good and evil." (Genesis 3:4-5.)

Satan says, "Your eyes will be open; you will be like God, you will know good and evil." Now watch how crafty his methods are. Will her eyes be opened? Yes. Will she know good and evil? Yes. Will that knowledge make her more like God? Yes; because she will be able to see and understand sin, which is something that God sees and understands. So these are all true statements! He has presented the words of God to Eve, and_manipulated them, knowing that Eve does not understand the full ramification of this distorted truth. Satan has taken the very words of God and used them against her. Notice how Eve verifies the success of this deception.

When the woman saw that the tree was good for food, and that it was a delight to the eyes, and that the tree was desirable to make one wise, she took from its fruit and ate; and she gave also to her husband with her, and he ate.

(Genesis 3:6.)

Eve basically says, "It can be eaten, it looks good and it will make me wise. I will be like God because I will be wise like Him." I believe that Eve is under the total deception that she can become more like God – the God who created her, the God who loves her – and what greater honor than to be more like this loving Father? She was deceived into thinking, by satan using God's very own words in the deception, that this was a good thing to become more like God. This shows how scary the stronghold of religion can be.

This same type of deception continues today. We are hungry for the Word of God and the enemy is presenting God's

Word in a distorted fashion to get us away from Him. We will ignore the instructions of God, we will ignore the consistency of Scripture, and we will ignore the context and the very character, principle and words of God, because we want a new revelation of Scripture.

Let me show you what I mean. Sometimes as a believer, we can be deceived just by our desire to have true biblical revelation. Revelation, by definition, is the point at which something that was hidden from us gets exposed for us to see. Revelation of Scripture is a dramatic moment when a mystery hidden for us in the Word of God gets revealed to us so that we have a heightened understanding. The enemy can place something out there that looks revelatory, so that we grab this "new understanding" and begin the application. One of the current day false revelations is something termed "free grace." Free grace, in a nutshell, is the application of a freedom to sin because grace is freely given. In other words, it's okay to sin, because you are under an applied grace. This is contradictory to the many Scriptures of the New Testament that instruct us to abolish sin in our lives. I won't take time in this book to cover my thoughts on free grace, but it has never made sense to me that when we are saved, we enter the Kingdom of God, and then say it's okay to continue to cross back over and play in the kingdom of darkness. We will listen to craziness if it is put in a spiritual package!

Was Eve wicked? No. She was sincere, but deceived. You can be a solid, loving, beautiful Christian and still be deceived.

And it was not Adam who was deceived, but the woman being deceived, fell into transgression.

(1 Timothy 2:14.)

Now put that with Genesis 3:6:

When the woman saw that the tree was good for food, and that it was a delight to the eyes, and that the tree was desirable to make one wise, she took from its fruit and ate; and she gave also to her husband with her, and he ate.

This verse tells us what Eve believed. She did not have a wicked bone in her body or the desire to disobey God; she sincerely believed this was a good thing to do. But ... she was deceived.

Let's look at Romans 5:14:

Nevertheless death reigned from Adam until Moses, even over those who had not sinned in the likeness of the offense of Adam, who is a type of Him who was to come.

Notice that this says death reigned from Adam until Moses. Wait, but didn't Eve sin first? Why did sin not reign from *Eve* until Moses?

Let's go back and look at Genesis 3:6-7:

When the woman saw that the tree was good for food, and that it was a delight to the eyes, and that the tree was desirable to make one wise, she took from its fruit and ate; and she gave also to her husband with her, and he ate. Then the eyes of both of them were opened, and they knew that they were naked; and they sewed fig leaves together and made themselves loin coverings.

Notice in this verse it says, "Then *the eyes...*" Or your version may say "And." Why does that sentence not start with "*So*, the eyes..." or "*Therefore*, the eyes..." rather than "*Then* the eyes ...?*" Because it was not until after *Adam* ate that their eyes were opened. Eve's eyes were not opened when she ate, and she believed she was doing a good thing when she gave to Adam so his eyes could be opened as well. Eve was deceived, but I believe Adam knew that what they were doing was wrong. I am not saying that it wasn't a sin for Eve; it was. But she was walking into it out of deception, and I do not believe Adam was deceived. First Timothy 2:14 specifically tells us that Adam was not deceived; that he willingly and knowingly took the fruit in rebellion to God's instruction.

When you take on the spiritual responsibility for others, it's an awesome and fearful responsibility. You must take it on with a legitimate reverence for the responsibility, because the reality of leading others spiritually includes the unfortunate possibility that, if *you* are deceived, you will lead others into sin. There are serious consequences for leading others into sin. Eve is deceived and leads Adam into the fall of man.

These things I have spoken to you so that you may be kept from stumbling. They will make you outcasts from the synagogue, but an hour is coming for everyone who kills you to think that he is offering service to God.
(John 16:1-2.)

Consider what is being said here. The deception is so great that these people are murdering each other and believing that they are doing it in service to God. They have read the Word of God. They believe they know the Word of God and they

149

believe that the Word of God gives them the right to commit murder. It's a startling example of the stronghold of religion and religious deception.

The stronghold of religion can also come through a spirit.

It happened that as we were going to the place of prayer, a slave-girl having a spirit of divination met us, who was bringing her masters much profit by fortune-telling. Following after Paul and us, she kept crying out, saying, "These men are bond-servants of the Most High God, who are proclaiming to you the way of salvation."

(Acts 16:16-17.)

Doesn't it seem like a good thing she is proclaiming? Isn't there truth in what she's saying? "Servants of God proclaiming salvation" seems like a truthful compliment to me. Wouldn't most of us be proud if someone was going before us proclaiming words like this about us? But look at Paul's response:

She continued doing this for many days. But Paul was greatly annoyed, and turned and said to the spirit, "I command you in the name of Jesus Christ to come out of her!" And it came out at that very moment.

(Acts 16:18.)

When Paul decides to address this as a problem, he says come out to the *spirit*. He doesn't speak to the woman; he speaks to the spirit *in* her. Now let me ask a question. How many of us, while we are preaching and proclaiming the salvation of Jesus Christ and someone compliments us on our efforts, would be astute enough to recognize that it is a spirit of

150

divination in that person? You see, we can have people in the church proclaiming the greatness of a pastor, speaker or evangelist and yet, they are operating under a demonic spirit trying to make a connection with us so that they can deceive us.

This is a tough subject, but how do we know whether someone is using the Word of God in a deceptive way or in a God honoring way? I think there are three ways of determining whether it is a righteous or deceptive use of Scripture.

One, always consider the source. My mentors will always be people who have walked with the Spirit for many, many years. If we are to take spiritual input from a source, let it be from someone who has walked with the Spirit and been taught by the Spirit for an extended period of time. You cannot meet someone, and in six months let him become a mentor to you. You have not seen his (or her) character under trial, in the dry times, or in the "drenched with the Spirit" times. You need to know how they walk, how they talk, and how they live out their Christianity before you let them speak into your life. Maybe, in simple terms, there is no such thing as a rookie expert. It does not exist. If you are looking for someone to speak into your life you need to ask the question, "Do I want expert advice or rookie advice?"

Listen, if you came to Christ six months ago and now you want to run a ministry at the church, reconsider it! You are too young in Christ. You are not ready to mentor others. The devil would have a field day with your pride, with your lack of wisdom, and with temptations. The devil would crush you like a bug! You need maturity. You have to have a track record of success to be ready for the higher things. That is why prophets measure prophets (1 Cor. 14:29). If we are going to get a word from God through a prophet, let's make sure we have some other more experienced prophets to measure that word, and to say yes that is from God, or no that is from their soul. That younger prophet believes they are hearing from God but in their zeal they have mixed their own words in with the word from God.

Two, hold what you're being taught up against the Word of God, AND the character of God. Eve was deceived when satan made eating the apple sound appealing, because he suggested it would make her be more like God. But his words did not match the character of God. Consider this – what did Paul see in the slave girl in Acts 16, that made him decide her behavior was not of God? He saw a slave, and that in and of itself is not bad. But he also saw that she was *selling* prophetic words. We don't see, in the character of God, that He sells His words to people. Paul saw others profiting from what the slave girl was doing. In other words, other people were using her to make money. He saw that her support became annoying. What do I mean by that? Have you ever been around someone who just has too much Jesus? Everything is Jesus. You feel "Jesus juked" on a regular basis. There comes a point when you realize someone is hiding behind his words about Jesus to try to look good. They don't have that relationship with Jesus, they just want you to believe they do. Paul recognized this lack of relationship in her. He recognized this in his spirit. He just knew something wasn't right, and her seemingly positive words became an irritant to him.

Three, know truth. As a new believer, you have come to know the truth about your lost condition and Christ's saving position. But it takes years to understand the full ramifications of justification, propitiation, identity in Christ, etc. So how do I know something is truth? Try considering the following:

1. Does this agree with the Word of God?

Do you find Scriptures that seem to disagree with what you think is truth? If so, there is a need to dig deeper until you get revelation on what the truth is.

2. Is it consistent with the character of God?

This is critical! You may not find a Scripture that directly answers your question, but you can measure your question against the character of God. Example: There is nothing in the Bible about whether or not we can smoke recreational marijuana. But the character of God says to be sober minded (First Cor. 15:34) and not given to drunkenness (Eph. 5:18). These verses do not address the actual issue, but when we consider why He says these things, we understand that His character is to not let something else be in control of our actions.

3. Is it confirmed in the Word in multiple places?

Over and over and over people take a Scripture out of context in order to conjure up some kind of support for what they want to believe. But if you are forced to make sure there are multiple places in Scripture that support your belief, you are less likely to be out of context.

4. Does it make spiritual sense?

We are supposed to walk in the Spirit. Things may make sense in the flesh, but make no sense in the Spirit. The easiest example is in giving. Giving your money to the Kingdom of God would indicate that you would end up with less money. But in the spiritual realm, giving is the key to opening up financial blessings. So you must assess things from a spiritual context and not just a physical one.

> ## 5. Does it contradict any of God's ways, including the order of God's ways?

Plenty of people want to operate out of God's order. A pastor is called of God to lead a church in direction "A." You come to the church with a desire to see God move in direction "B." Because of your great desire, you tell the pastor he needs to move in direction "B", but you have forgotten that God put the pastor in place and the pastor is responsible to God for direction "A." He is not responsible to *you* for direction "B."

> ## 6. Can it be confirmed through mentors?

We need to seek advice about what we believe from mature believers before we go around spouting our ideas. This one simple step will save a lot of embarrassment when you learn that you were wrong in what you believed. Often, a young believer comes and tells me this amazing revelation they got from a scripture, but it is not a revelation at all.

Let me give you a recent example. A man called me and said, "I learned today that you cannot go to heaven unless you are water baptized and baptized in the Spirit." So I responded, "Interesting. What Scripture are you using for that revelation?" He said, "John chapter 3, where Jesus says, 'To enter the kingdom of God you must be born of the water and the Spirit.'" It took only a few moments to remind him that in this Scripture,

Nicodemus was asking the question, "How can I enter a second time into my mother's womb?" but Jesus responded with "What is flesh is flesh and what is spirit is spirit." Then he understood that Jesus was saying you were born of your mother's womb (born of the water from the womb,) but the born-again experience was of the Spirit (when your spirit is regenerated by the Holy Spirit at salvation). Mentors can save you a lot of learning time and some embarrassment along the way.

7. Is it advice from a rookie – yourself included?

Let me be clear. If you are a rookie in Christ, a rookie in theology, a rookie in doctrine, a rookie in marriage, a rookie in child rearing, a rookie in baseball, or a rookie in anything, you are not ready to give expert advice. God loves you and has great plans for you. God is preparing your future even as we speak. You may well be the next Billy Graham or Smith Wigglesworth, but you are not that today. A rookie can indeed speak truth. I am not saying they can't. But rookies need nurturing, discipleship, and maturity. What I'm saying is that when you are considering something you have heard, you need to know the source, and whether or not that source is qualified to give you good advice.

I started in ministry as an eighth-grade boys' Sunday school teacher. I thank God that someone had the wisdom to give me a lower position so I could learn how to teach people, I could learn how to put a lesson together, I could learn how to preach. They gave me a curriculum. They said, "Stay with this, do not go with your own material. You need to learn from others before you are ready to write your own lessons." In other words, through these people's tutelage, I learned the pitfalls of teaching before I was put in front of a congregation of more mature adults where I could potentially have embarrassed myself by not being ready to teach.

I want to remind you again that if you take on a position of spiritual responsibility for others, this has serious consequences. Do not take this position lightly! Take it on with fear and trembling.

The stronghold that hides the spirit of religion can also come through misguided sincerity. This was the problem with the Pharisees who get such a bad rap in Scripture. Although they deserved what Jesus said to them, it is hard not to argue that many of them paid a very high price to be a Pharisee. This position was a lifetime dedication. Part of their learning process was to memorize the Torah. Most of us today consider ourselves good if we can accurately quote a dozen Scriptures, much less five complete books. They were earnestly following God but had completely lost sight of His character, which is apparent in so many of the Scriptures. For example, they wanted to punish the woman caught in adultery, and Jesus said no. They wanted to condemn Jesus for healing someone on the Sabbath. They condemn the disciples for plucking grains of wheat and eating them on the Sabbath. They *believed* they were following the code of God in their accusations. But listen, you can be one hundred percent right in your biblical understanding, and one hundred percent wrong in your application of that understanding. Let me repeat that. You can be one hundred percent right in your biblical understanding, and one hundred percent wrong in your application of that understanding. That is what the Pharisees did. They knew the Word. They did all of this out of their zeal for God but they were deceived about the character of God. Jesus said to them,

"Hey – wasn't the Sabbath rest made for man? Man was not created to appease the Sabbath. The Sabbath was made to minister to man – not the other way around. Hey – if your donkey fell in a ditch on the Sabbath, you would get it out, right? Hey! Can you not rejoice that this man was healed?! Instead you want him to be sick until you approve of a time for his healing? That's messed up! You don't understand God's love for this man!" Jesus was saying that the character of God is love! Express love first! *That* is in line with the character of God.

Even today, the spirit of religion can be seen from a mile away. The spirit of religion says for everything there must be a rule, and anyone not following the rule must be condemned. Remember this is what the Pharisees did and, for it, Jesus called them hypocrites because even *they* could not follow the rules they wanted to enforce.

I recall addressing the spirit of religion many times in the church setting. One time a man came to the church I was pastoring and told me that scripture says if we are not bowing, and face down on the floor, then we're not worshipping. He quoted the scripture in which satan tells Jesus in the wilderness, to "bow down" and worship him. He told me that nothing stands in the throne room of God, so if people weren't bowing, or on the floor, then they were not worshipping. I explained to this religious spirit that God does not look on the outward appearance of man; He looks upon the heart. And I said that we must worship in *spirit* and in truth, not in the flesh and in truth. To be clear, we may indeed bow and get on the floor, but God is not looking at our physical position; He's looking for a bowed down spirit, a contrite heart. What this man wanted was to control worshippers with his deceived understanding of

Scripture and his fleshly application.

At another time, I was helping a church move from a traditional worship format (piano and organ only) to a contemporary worship format (guitars, drums, keyboards, etc.). Without getting technical, in order to do that we had to move from their simple PA sound system to a more complex mixing board. That mixing board had to be at ground level in the sanctuary, so we had to build a sound booth in the sanctuary. We accomplished that without giving up a single seat or blocking anyone's view of the stage, and we built it so that it would blend into the walls of the room. But an eighty-year-old building committee member, in anger, literally put his finger in my face and said, "Your sound booth is a pimple on the face of God's sanctuary!" Biting my tongue, I calmly explained that First Corinthians 3:16 asks the question, "Do you not know that you are the temple of God and that the Spirit of God dwells in you?" I said, "This is a room where we gather to worship; God's sanctuary is *you!*"

Most people with a stronghold of religion are dead serious people. They are deceived into believing they are defending God. You have to love them, but at the same time find a way to address that spirit of religion. I have been a believer for thirty-six years and a Bible teacher for thirty-two years. I can tell you that some things I believed and taught in my late twenties, I no longer believe or teach. So much of what I taught and believed then came from the spirit of religion, in both traditions and incorrect teaching I was listening to, and I was not mature enough to measure or examine it myself.

The spirit of religion shuns humility. The spirit of religion has no need to show grace. It wants only to enforce a rule.

Now Saul, still breathing threats and murder against the disciples of the Lord, went to the high priest, and asked for letters from him to the synagogue at Damascus, so that if he found any belonging to the Way, both men and women, he might bring them bound to Jerusalem.

(Acts 9:1-2.)

Saul was a Pharisee. Here he is asking for a letter from the high priest to give him authority to go to Damascus and bring back for trial in Jerusalem anyone who believes in Jesus as Messiah. Saul's life was serving God. He was a well-educated man. He dedicated his life to following God. And yet here, he is ready to arrest, bring to trial, and possibly put to death anyone following Jesus! Saul is deceived. The Pharisees never understood the Word of God enough to understand that Jesus was the long-awaited Messiah. They had memorized the Scriptures that spoke of Jesus, where He would be born, what His lineage would be, and how to identify Him; but they were deceived. They were convinced they were right before God. Isn't it amazing how we can see the error in others but not in ourselves?

So, what are the lies that are hiding in our belief system when it comes to religion?

> 1. When I defend the things of God to others, I don't have to be loving in doing so.

This cannot be done before God. You will never get your message through with a sledgehammer. All you will get is defensiveness, disunity, and division if you can't deliver the truth in love.

159

> 2. Love and unity are less important than being right.

When you take this posture, you are sitting in the seat of judgment because you believe you are right.

> 3. Everyone should be at the same level of understanding that I am.

The religious stronghold will make someone say things like, "Don't you see this in Scripture? Its right there! It is so clear, how can you not get it?" when the person *themselves* did not understand it last year. But now that they do, they insist you must understand it the way they do. Why can we not give others grace for not understanding what we ourselves didn't understand only a short time ago? You may actually be mature in your understanding. But listen, we can only *deliver* the word of God; it is the Holy Spirit who will *teach* the other person. Without the conviction of the Holy Spirit, we are just professing words that land on deaf ears. So if you have a problem with their lack of understanding, take it up with the Holy Spirit!

> 4. God would be proud of me for pointing out the sins of others.

If we confront in love, there is no judgment or condemnation, so humility is a key in battling the stronghold of religion. You have to ask yourself, "Could I be wrong?" Just because I think I understand, I could still be wrong. Eve thought she understood what the fruit would do for her, but she was deceived; she was wrong.

One of the signs of being a mature believer is, knowing when not to speak. When you are actually mature, you can recognize that the other person is not yet ready to receive what you're about to say. And if they can't receive it now, why are you saying it? One acronym that I think would help every believer is, WAIT (which we talk more about in the chapter on the Stronghold of Gossip). This WAIT does not mean to hold off before you speak. It's an acronym that means, Why Am I Talking? If we ask ourselves that question more often, we might be showing that by *not* speaking, we have wisdom – rather than by speaking proving, we have none.

If you want to identify the stronghold of religion in another person, here is what you look for. They do not show love, they show judgment and condemnation. They want to embarrass, expose and damage the people whom they believe are offenders. They are prideful and un-teachable. They are critical and accusing. And they must convince others that their view is right and the other person's is wrong. In other words, it's important for them to be seen by the majority as right in their condemnation of someone. Listen, it is a fine line between the Word of God and the stronghold of religion.

This stronghold should not exist in the church. That is not who we should be to each other as believers.

By this all men will know that you are My disciples, if you have love for one another.

(John 13:35.)

161

Jesus is saying here "By this – by what I am about to tell you – all men (*all* men) will know you are following Me." He is saying that everyone on the planet will know we are disciples of Jesus. Here is the one thing that will be evidence that we are His: if we have love for one another.

Most of the time, a person who is working within the stronghold of religion is not looking for reconciliation; they are looking for separation. They are identifying the people they believe need to be shunned or removed, because they, the person with the stronghold of religion, believe those people are unfit to be among the believers.

Maybe what we need to do is to begin looking for fruit. Scripture says, a good tree will be known by good fruit, and a bad tree by bad fruit (Luke 6:43). A religious stronghold bears the following fruit: gossip, out of order actions, judgment, immaturity, rumors, division, taking sides, and disunity. Another subtle fruit of the stronghold of religion may be charm. Obviously, the fruit we *should* see is reconciliation and restoration! Any disunity in the body should break our hearts. The desire for unity should come running to the fore! When someone among us is operating in the stronghold of religion, we owe it to them to go to them and say, "Brother/Sister, I see and hear judgment and condemnation coming out of you." The Bible lays out a process to follow, whereby we go to our fellow Christians *one on one* in an attempt to resolve the problem (Matt 18:15). It does not say to go with your posse, or in front of everyone you want to impress. It does not say to go with the people whom you want to see the error of you brother's way. The Bible says to go to them in private. And if that does not work, take someone with you -- someone who can be neutral – someone who may end up saying that *you* are wrong. Because if we are not willing to take someone who may say we are wrong, our pride is at work. Then finally, He says in Matt. 18:17, that if you cannot resolve it, take it to the church. I do not believe He is recommending the church take a vote. I think what He is saying is that there are mature spiritual leaders at your church who can help get this reconciled.

As believers, we have the common desire to live in unity under God's truth. Unfortunately, that process falls apart when someone decides it is *his* job to point out other peoples' wrongs, and is deceived into thinking he should make that judgment. We have to be willing to search the Scriptures and humble ourselves to learn. We have to realize that we are each accountable to God for what we believe and for how we treat others. And we must guard against the deception and lies that are hiding in the stronghold of religion. Remember to judge the tree (your belief) by its fruit. The fruit of the spirit of religion is judgment and condemnation, but the fruit of the Spirit of truth is gentleness and love.

About The Author

Does he have a seminary degree? Has he pastored several churches? Does he have a loving family with believing children? Is he currently pastoring a large church? And has he sacrificed much for the cause of Christ? These are some of the questions people have asked about the author – and the answer to all of these questions is yes. But the bottom line is that Todd Mozingo is a spirit filled, apostolic teacher, who wants to see the church put the Word of God back together with the Spirit of God, so that the local church can be a powerful place for people to encounter the Living God for themselves. Currently serving as the founder and lead pastor of Revive Church in South Florida – a church passionately pursuing the early church that we read about in the book of Acts – Todd's desire is to see the divide between the Fundamentalists and the Pentecostals erased, and the church at large brought back to a place where the Bible and the Holy Spirit can work in unity together, incorporating a solid doctrine with miraculous power.

98492393R00098

Made in the USA
Columbia, SC
27 June 2018